The Language of Love

The Language of Love

A Basic Christian Vocabulary

C. FRANKLIN BROOKHART

RESOURCE *Publications* • Eugene, Oregon

THE LANGUAGE OF LOVE
A Basic Christian Vocabulary

Copyright © 2018 Franklin C. Brookhart. All rights reserved. Except for brief quotations in critical publications or reviews, no part of this book may be reproduced in any manner without prior written permission from the publisher. Write: Permissions, Wipf and Stock Publishers, 199 W. 8th Ave., Suite 3, Eugene, OR 97401.

Resource Publications
An Imprint of Wipf and Stock Publishers
199 W. 8th Ave., Suite 3
Eugene, OR 97401

www.wipfandstock.com

PAPERBACK ISBN: 978-1-5326-5060-4
HARDCOVER ISBN: 978-1-5326-5061-1
EBOOK ISBN: 978-1-5326-5062-8

Manufactured in the U.S.A. 08/31/18

All scripture quotations herein are from the New Revised Standard Version Bible, copyright© 1989 by the Division of Christian Education of the National Council of Churches of Christ in the U.S.A. All rights reserved.

I dedicate this work to the Glory of God
and the advancement of the Reign of Jesus Christ.

Contents

1. **Apocalypse** — 1
   Unveiling God's Future
2. **Atonement** — 6
   Setting Things Right
3. **Bible** — 13
   The B-I-B-L-E, That's the Book for Me
4. **Catholic** — 21
   The Whole Thing
5. **Church** — 25
   You Can't Be a Christian Alone
6. **Cross** — 29
   Love, Not Power
7. **Doctrine and Dogma** — 34
   Teaching and Learning
8. **Faith** — 38
   What Do I Trust?
9. **Forgiveness** — 44
   The Healing of Relationships
10. **Gifts of the Spirit** — 50
    Open your Gifts!
11. **God** — 56
    Above and Beyond
12. **Grace** — 63
    Better Than I Deserve

13. Holy Baptism — 68
The Waters of Grace

14. Holy Eucharist — 73
The Gifts of God for the People of God

15. Holy Spirit — 78
The Breath of God

16. Holy Trinity — 82
God Is Not Simple

17. Hope — 87
God's Future

18. Incarnation — 91
God Made Flesh

19. Jesus — 96
What's in a Name?

20. Justification — 102
Getting Right with God

21. Love — 107
All We Need Is Love

22. Mystery — 111
Into the Depths of God

23. Ordination — 114
Leadership and Service in Christ's Church

24. Resurrection — 119
The Victory of God

25. Revelation — 122
Unveiling the Unknown

26. Sacraments — 127
Visible and Invisible

27. Sacrifice — 134
What We Offer to God

28. Salvation — 141
To Be Safe and Sound

29. Sin   145
    More Than Missing the Mark

30. Worship   149
    What Is God Worth?

Acknowledgments

I AM GRATEFUL TO General Theological Seminary in New York City and its Dean and President, the Very Rev. Kurt H. Dunkle, for graciously providing accommodations during the research stage of this book. Dean Dunkle opened the Christoph Keller Jr Library for my use, where I was ably assisted by Patrick Cater, Library Manager, and Caitlin Stamm, Reference Librarian. I thank Dean Dunkle and his wife for the warm personal hospitality extended me.

I am also grateful to the School of Theology of the University of the South, Sewanee, TN, and its Dean and Vice-President, the Rt. Rev. J. Neil Alexander, for kindly allowing me to serve as Bishop-in-Residence while I did research for this work. Bishop Alexander provided accommodations and welcomed me to the theological library of the seminary, where Romulus D. Stefanut, Theological Librarian, was quite helpful to me. Bishop Alexander offered warm southern hospitality, and I thank him for that.

I acknowledge the assistance of the Rev. Canon C.K. Robertson, Canon to the Presiding Bishop and Primate of The Episcopal Church, for his help, encouragement, and interest in all of my books. He has been an inspiration to me, and I value his support.

I offer a special and heartfelt thanks to my wife Susan. An accomplished and prolific author herself, she has always supported me in my writing efforts and has allowed me time to work on this and my other books. I am always grateful to her.

Introduction

I was sitting in my miniature wooden chair in the Sunday School room. I was ten years old and attending Vacation Bible School. The teacher posed this question: what is grace. It was part of the Bible verse we were memorizing that day. I had sung "Amazing Grace" in church, and I knew several women in the parish with that name. But I did not know the meaning of the term. I had no answer for the teacher.

This little example, I hope, points out that Christians have a special vocabulary, indeed, an especially rich and profound one. These items of "church talk" serve as quick points of reference for ideas, event, and persons of significant importance to the lives of Christian people. They are key words, which open doors of understanding, wisdom, and experience.

In this book I propose to explore some of the most important of these words. I hope to help readers build a basic vocabulary of terms that the Church has used throughout its long history. Thus, I offer a series of essays with the hope that an understanding of the language of love will lead to a more lively and transformational faith in the God revealed by Jesus Christ.

I sometimes hear people say, "We Christians, and preachers in particular, ought to speak in terms that are clear and understandable by all." To that I reply that we should sense no need to apologize for using a unique vocabulary. Indeed, every endeavor develops its own "talk." Baseball people, for example, speak of "showing bunt" or "that player is in scoring position." Cooks talk about "folding in eggs" or "blanching vegetables." These are the technical terms used in those activities. Christians, too, speak in our own unique language. We are, after all, dealing with such matters as the nature of God and the complexities of the human heart, and on these occasions, we necessarily make use of our vocabulary.

Most of the important terms used by the Church are rooted in scripture and have a long history of application. So, I will in each essay make some reference to the Bible. I do this in part because the scriptures stand

Introduction

as authoritative for us, but also because the stories in the Bible can offer deep insights into the how and why of our behavior. Additionally in some cases, I take a quick look at both the etymology of terms and at their usage in our Christian tradition. I will also tap into my own experience as a baptized person and as a bishop, and at the end of each section will include some questions to help launch your own engagement with the word under consideration

A quick look at the Table of Contents shows that I have not attempted to be comprehensive, but the words I have included are in my experience both foundational to an understanding of the Christian faith and also are often subject to misunderstanding. Please do not see this book as a complete theological dictionary. But please do see it as one person's carefully considered meditations about living into the Paschal Mystery, about loving Jesus, and about being a citizen of both this world and the Reign of God. Feel free to read the book in any order.

The contents of some essays overlap at bit, but I hope that only encourages you to read further.

I hope our time together will result in a deeper or more lively relationship with our Risen Lord for you. So, let's get started.

chapter 1

Apocalypse
Unveiling God's Future

IF YOU ENTER THE word "apocalypse" into Google, here are some of the entries you will find:

- a Marvel comic book super villain,
- a bunker built by the wealthy to prepare for global diaster,
- signs of environmental doom,
- and five reasons why a zombie apocalypse could happen.

The word clearly has entered the popular vocabulary, and carries with it a variety of nuances. The general use suggests an expectation of imminent doom and the reasons for such an expectation. It has become almost synonymous with "diaster."

My wife and I used to watch a television show that revealed the secrets of magic tricks. A person would perform the illusion as the audience would see it, and then would come a commercial. After that the announcer would solemnly say, "And now the reveal," and the trick would then be explained. The word "apocalypse" simply means to reveal or to uncover. In the Bible what is revealed is the circumstances leading to the fulfillment of God's plan for humanity. An apocalypse uncovers what God intends to do.

The last book in the Bible is today generally called "Revelation" (not Revelations) or "The Revelation to St. John the Divine." But another title of long usage is "The Apocalypse." The first verse says it well: "The revelation (in Greek, the apocalypse) of Jesus Christ, which God gave to him to his servants what must soon take place; he made it known by sending his angel to his servant John." That is, the book unveils what must soon take place under God's providence.

Now we hone in on the meaning of the term. More specifically, apocalypse is a form of literature; it is a genre. The Bible stands as a library, a collection of various books in a number of genres from different historical periods. To some that seems obvious, but that fact needs attention. The reason I emphasize that is because we understand what we read through our sense of genre. For example, when we look at a newspaper we do not read a sports article the same way we read an editorial. We approach the comics differently than news articles. Without thinking about it, we know that an editorial is someone's opinion and that a news story lays before us the facts of an event. It's all a matter of genre.

We should approach scripture in a similar way. We read the Psalms as poetry with all that that implies. But we read the letters of Paul understanding that it is correspondence addressing specific people in a certain place.

The genre of apocalypse arose as a common form of literature in late Judaism and early Christianity (about 300 BC till about 150 AD). The people of the time knew the form and how to understand it. Most of these works are now historical curiosities, but several have become a part of the church's life and literature. Mark 13, sometimes called the Little Apocalypse, serves as an instance. Parts of the Old Testament book of Daniel, and bits of the New Testament (2 Thessalonians 2.1-20), are further examples, the major instance being, of course, the book of Revelation.

The purpose of an apocalypse is to interpret a crisis which the people of God are facing. This genre grows out of a setting in which it seems as if the world is falling apart and as if evil appears to be prevailing against the forces of order and godliness. Authors of apocalypse did this by using highly metaphorical language. Numerology, codes, angels and demons play important roles; and earthly rulers and powers are presented in veiled form. We today function is similar ways. When we see a picture of or read about Uncle Sam we know that that is a veiled reference to the United States. Our national emblem shows an eagle holding thunderbolts and olive branches, suggesting a noble nation with power to seek peace. We should approach any apocalypse with a similar turn of mind.

In a moment we will look at Revelation as a case study of apocalypse. But first, I ask that you put aside a popular notion about that book. Some see it as a code book about what is about the happen today. So, they read it and then look for signs of the times that fit what they read. My response to that method is a question. Why would early Christians have preserved Revelation and considered it holy scripture if its setting was actually the twenty-first century? If that were the case it would have been nonsense to those early believers. In fact, they read, used, and preserved it because it spoke a word of God to them in their situation. It is not a book about what is about to happen in the Middle East today, but rather what happened in the Middle East in the first century.

In Christian scripture and tradition the Revelation to St. John the Divine stands as the primary instance of apocalypse. The writer says his name is John, and calls himself simply a servant of Jesus and a brother to other Christians. He functions as a prophet in the Old Testament sense, a person called to proclaim a message from God. He does not speak of himself as an evangelist, so we should not think of him as the author of the gospel of John. Nor is he the apostle John, son of Zebedee. John was a common name then, and we should not confuse the three John's we encounter in the New Testament. There are: John the Apostle, John the Evangelist, and John the Divine. Our guy is the final person on the list.

The John of the Apocalypse, sometimes referred to as St. John the Divine, received a divine word while on the Island of Patmos, a small and rugged outcropping in the Aegean Sea. The church's tradition states that he was banished there by the Roman authorities. Here is what John himself writes: "I, John. Your brother who share with you in Jesus the persecution and the kingdom and the patient endurance, was on the island called Patmos because of the word of God and the testimony of Jesus. I was in the spirit on the Lord's day, and I heard behind me a loud voice like a trumpet saying, 'Write in a book what you see and send it to the seven churches, to Ephesus, to Smyrna, to Pergamum, to Thyatira, to Sardis, to Philadelphia, and to Laodicea.'" (Revelation 1. 9-10)

This passage implies that John had been exiled because he was preaching the gospel. In about 95 AD the Roman emperor Domitian initiated persecutions and harassment of Christians throughout his empire. In the text, John notes these persecutions, and elsewhere he writes of arrests (2.10), and says that one believer, Antipas, has already been martyred (2.13).

There were seven churches in what today we call Turkey, and John had some sort of association with them. He himself has suffered the harassment of arrest and the anxiety about possible martyrdom, and he shares these factors with the seven churches as well. The first part of Revelation contains seven letters, one to each of the above church (chapters 2 and 3). And his prophetic word to each he takes a carrot-and-stick approach. He congratulates each for some good qualities and works. For example, the people of Ephesus he commends for their endurance and their ability to identify false apostles. He states, "But this I have against you, that you have abandoned the love you had at first." (2.4) Each letter unfolds in this manner.

After the seven letters, the scope of the work expands to a cosmic level. "After this I looked, and there in heaven a door stood open!" (4.1) Led by a heavenly being, John is allowed to witness a series of visions, all carefully wrought and beautifully composed. We are soon presented to the main actors in a cosmic struggle between good and evil, the One who sits upon the throne and the Lamb who was slain and yet lives. These, of course, refer to God and to the Risen Christ. The enemy is the dragon who dwells in Babylon, that is, the emperor and the Roman empire. The heavenly struggles mirror the Christians' experience with their government, a sharp battle between God and God's people with the forces of evil and persecution. In the end the dragon is defeated and cast into the lake of fire (19. 17-21) The book closes with a glorious vision of the new creation, where God's people dwell in the very presence of God and where nothing accursed is found there.

The point of the vision is to encourage the Christians in the seven churches to endure with courage and hope, knowing that in the end the victory belongs to God. While the book does not overtly state it, this confidence is rooted in the resurrection of Christ, which proves that nothing can separate God's people from the love of God witnessed in Jesus Christ.

Throughout this work John uses typical apocalyptic devices. Visions of heaven, angels of God who carry out the will of God, and strange and otherworldly creatures like something out of science fiction. There are exalted hymns of praise. The universe is painted as a dualistic struggle between extreme evil and the perfect goodness of God. Through it all the constant refrain proclaims the victory of God. The book constantly exhorts the baptized to endure patiently the present struggles confident of the eventual triumph of the One who sits upon the throne and of the Lamb.

At first glance biblical apocalypse appears to be impenetrable and chaotic. But if we understand how to read it, a strong message of hope and encouragement emerges. We can do no better than to quote one of the heavenly hymns penned by John: "Now have come the salvation and the power and the kingdom of our God and the authority of his Messiah, for the accusers of our comrades has been thrown down…they have conquered him by the blood of the Lamb and by the word of their testimony… Rejoice, then, you heavens and those who dwell in them" (12. 10-12)

DISCUSSION QUESTIONS

First, do you think you could describe today's world in terms of a struggle between good and evil? If so, what examples would you use?

Second, if you were to compose an apocalypse what current symbols, signs, and characters might you use?

Third, Jesus' resurrection stands at the center of every New Testament apocalypse. How can you promote the primacy of his resurrection in your life and in the life of your church?

Fourth, where today can you see the victory of God dawning?

chapter 2

Atonement
Setting Things Right

I WAS SIXTEEN, AND had just been granted a driver's license. I was backing the car out of the garage. For reasons I still do not understand I had left the car door partly open. That meant that I smashed the car door into the metal track that held up the garage door. Double trouble! I had in my haste damaged both the car and the garage. When I informed my father I could see fury cross his face, but to his credit he said nothing. But I felt awful. The question that kept crossing my mind was this: how could I set things right with my dad.

That is the issue of atonement. How can I set things right for damage done? In the church the term is used primarily about the marred and injured relationship between God and humanity, but it certainly pertains also to human-human and human-environmental bonds. Can repairs be made? What does that cost us? How can we make up for shattering the important connections that make us human beings?

The Sunday School definition for atonement is simple. It means" at-one-ment." It refers to the process of taking the broken pieces of relationships and putting them back together. But it is easier said than done, isn't it? This morning I had a soft-boiled egg for breakfast. The result was a broken egg shell laying in the kitchen sink. It would be virtually impossible to put the fragile pieces of the broken shell together again. Similarly, the bonds connecting God and humanity and person to person are as fragile and easily shattered as that egg.

But work at atonement we must. We will spend the rest of our lives dealing with the errors, the mistakes, the anger, and the intentional and unintentional harm done by our actions, attitudes, and words. We all leave behind a trail pain and brokenness.

God enters the picture when we remember that God is the primary relationship we have. God is the one in whom and by whom we live and move and have our being. Part of the character of God revealed in holy scripture is that God loves relationships. God longs to be connected to persons and to the world, both of which are the result of divine creation and of God's continued action to sustain the whole of creation. Furthermore, the doctrine of the Trinity suggests that God is a community of three persons perfectly united by love. So, God is relationship.

The concept of atonement acknowledges a truth that we do not often want to face, namely, that as persons and as a race we injure, break, and maim all the relationships in which we live, including our primary connection with God. And we have our ways of trying to ameliorate the resulting sense of shame and guild. One common method says that we call the brokenness an accident. It just happened, we say. I did not intend any harm. It was simply an unfortunate mishap. I suppose that we need to concede the possibility of accidents. But I well remember as a college student working for a company that emphasized safety; one of their slogans was that there was no such thing as an accident. Even if accidents are a genuine possibility, the hurt, the pain, the shame, and the guilt remain, and, therefore, need to be dealt with.

We also try to side-step our role in ruining relationships by pleading ignorance and by blaming others. I have done both more often than I want to admit, but I also know deep in my heart that these are usually feeble attempts to shift blame. For whatever the reason, I do damage my relationship with God and with others, even the people I love most.

All this has a merry-go-round quality, doesn't it? We do and say that same, old, injurious things, feel the same guilt, and the pain we have caused haunts us. Even our attempts at atonement sometimes feel like a sham, because want to escape the consequences or make ourselves look better than we have been. The result? Atonement and integrity we so much seek and need seem unattainable.

Just at that place we stand with the anguished apostle Paul. He writes, "I do not understand my own actions. For I do not do what I want, but I do the very thing I hate . . . I can will what is right, but I cannot do it. . . .

Wretched man that I am! Who will rescue me from this body of death?" (Romans 7: 15, 18, 24)

The answer to Paul's question is that God can and does set things right through Jesus Christ. God, the only being who lives the perfect integrity of holiness, the only being who does not stand in need of atonement, the only being whose existence is not contingent on being in any relationship, always seek to establish a living connection with all creation, especially humanity. I believe we can state the astonishing fact that God's work of atonement stands as both the basis of and the living heart of the universe.

God's atoning activity shines most brightly in the death and the resurrection of Jesus Christ. Another way to state this is: God was active in Jesus, because Jesus was the very embodiment of God operating in the human sphere of time and space. The scriptures use many metaphors in an attempt to describe how the cross brings about atonement. Here is a list: reconciliation, expiation, redemption, ransom, and justification. These function as virtual synonyms for atonement, and all point to the mystery of the meaning of Jesus' death.

At this point we need to stop and state four important factors. If we are not clear about these matters we will find ourselves in a theological and existential quagmire. First, atonement is the work of God. God initiates it, and it is rooted in the character and nature of God. In one of the earliest divine self-disclosures in the biblical story, God speaks the sacred divine name "YHWH" (translated into English as the word LORD). It describes God's character: " The LORD, the LORD, a God merciful and gracious, slow to anger, and abounding in steadfast love and faithfulness, keeping steadfast love for the thousandth generation, forgiving iniquity and transgression and sin." (Exodus 34: 6-7) Because of who God is, God chooses to make atonement with us, and God does this out of God's steadfast love.

Second, God works atonement through Christ. The church has never tried to limit its understanding of how the cross accomplishes atonement, but has, instead, used a variety of images and metaphors to probe the mysteries of Jesus' crucifixion. Furthermore, the church always connects the cross with the resurrection. Easter stands as the mark of divine approval of Jesus' death and establishes that the life and steadfast love of God conquers all that separates us God, all that would undo the work of atonement.

Third, none of the metaphors should be interpreted to suggest that Christ's death was to appease God. I too often hear statements that put forward the image of Jesus as God's whipping boy. Sometimes called the theory of penal substitutionary atonement, this view presents a cruel and morally offensive divinity. And it certainly betrays the biblical view of God's character, and, therefore, represents a disagreeable misreading of the Bible.

Four, metaphors are only metaphors, analogies based on experience. They cannot be pressed too hard. For instance, Jesus' death can be described as an atoning ransom. We are familiar with that word and what it suggests. A ransom is paid to set another person free. If we push this, we end up in strange places: Jesus' death was a fee paid to the Devil in order to free humanity, as one theory puts it. This raises more questions than it answers, does it not? For me the term connotes Jesus' shouldering the burden of God's commitment to deal with humanity in terms of mercy and love. Images suggest similarity and not exact likenesses.

A sacramental mind-set helps in working with atonement images. We should not think that atonement is a mind-game God plays. For example, the Old Testament brims with statements that God forgives, that God accepts human beings. But that is concretized, made real, sacramentalized, by actions and events. In a sense we all live in the "show me" state of Missouri. We want to see the proof. Because the atonement was worked out in time and space, in the person Jesus, it becomes really real for us.

My late father-in-law loved jigsaw puzzles. He would throw out the pieces on the dining room table, and everyone in the family was invited to take part in putting it together.

I wish to throw out some pieces of scripture, so that we together can work at forming a biblical picture of atonement. We will piece together various images and metephors in order to get a sense of the scriptures' view of atonement.

First, we look at Isaiah 52:13-53.12. I suggest you read the whole passage, but I will quote only bits and pieces for the sake of our work together. This text speaks of a "suffering servant," whose very suffering accomplishes God's mission. I believe it is significant that this text is read in its entirety on Good Friday when we focus on the death of Jesus and its meaning. By way of background, understand that the prophet Isaiah had the nation of Israel in mind when he speaks of "my servant." The sufferings of Israel at the hands of the Babylonians was regarded as sacrificial service that would benefit all nations. But like most biblical texts, this one makes many connections with the human story. So, the church has always seen the suffering servant above all others as Jesus, who in his own person epitomized the people of God.

Note especially this passage: "He was despised and rejected by others, a man of suffering and acquainted with infirmity.... surely, he has borne our infirmities and carried our diseases." (Is. 53. 3-4)

God was active in Christ, sharing in the woundedness of humanity. He knew our suffering and infirmity.

The irony is that the pain and rejection he endured was not of his making. Yet, he accepted it, absorbed it, and made it his own. That constitutes an act of profound commitment to and solidarity with humanity. The crux of the sacrifice of the cross lies in Jesus' sharing all that troubles us and robs us of life and love.

I have two daughters, both adults now. When they were young my wife and I shared in their colds, ear infections, stomach flu. We set aside our own comfort in order to comfort them. We sat with them in the middle of the night, cleaned up messes, and paid doctor bills. This is nothing more than any good parent would do, but it was a sacrifice of love that was generated by commitment to our daughters. The cross is all this writ large. The first piece, then, pictures sacrifice for others, a sacrifice the results in healing for those who suffer.

The New Testament book of Hebrews presents Jesus as the fulfilment of the Old Testament's system of atoning sacrifice. The Hebrew scriptures describe in detail many ceremonies involving the sacrifice of animals, grain, and incense. These were offered to God in the Jerusalem Temple in order to set things right with God, to make atonement for sins committed. In part the Israelites appear to have seen this as a form of appeasement, but in a deeper sense they were offering to God something valuable in order to demonstrate their seriousness about maintaining a relationship with God.

The New Testament book of Hebrews, however, describes God's great reversal. "Unlike other high priests, [Jesus] has no need to offer sacrifices day after day, first for his own sins, and then for those of the people; this he did once for all when he offered himself." (Hebrews 7.27) The astonishing imagery here says that God provides God's own self as the sacrifice that establishes atonement. Would it be pressing the image too far to say that God makes a sacrifice to humanity as the ultimate sign of divine commitment to and seriousness about maintaining relationship? If religion is understood as humanity's quest for God, then this image turns religion upside-down. Here God offers God's own self in the person of Jesus to signify divine seriousness and commitment to humanity. Thus, we can add another piece to the puzzle

Closely related to the ideas of the above two passages is 2 Corinthians 5. 19: "In Christ God was reconciling the world to himself, not counting their trespasses against them." The connections between God and humanity are repaired, pulled back together as the result of the sacrifice of God's own self. The passage continues to amaze by declaring that the church no less carries on the work of God's reconciliation by participating in the Christ's self-sacrifice.

A Latin-based word, "reconcile" connotes connecting something that has been separated. So, we have a third piece to add to our theological jigsaw puzzle. This picture shows Christ making God's plea of reconciliation to the world. Part of a collect for mission from the Book of Common Prayer expresses this wonderfully well. "Lord Jesus Christ, you stretched out your arms of love on the hard wood of the cross that everyone might come within the reach of your saving embrace." (p. 101) We can now add the reconciliation piece to the puzzle.

Moving on with Paul again adds to our picture of atonement. "For while we were still weak, at the right time Christ died for the ungodly.... God proves his love for us in that while we still were sinners Christ died for us." (Romans 5. 6, 8) I need to post a warning sign here. In this passage "Christ died for us" does not mean "in place of" or "in our stead.". These phrases represent an all-to-common slant of this key verse. Rather, these phrases denote purpose. That is, we are the object of God's atoning purpose in Christ's work on the cross. The overriding idea is that the cross proves God's love for us. Again, the seriousness and loyalty of God to humanity is set forth on the cross. That point receives more emphasis by the fact that human beings just like us had demonstrated their rupture with the divine by perpetrating Jesus's suffering; they acted as enemies of God. But Jesus breaks the perpetual cycle of vengeance and anger by accepting suffering. This is the cosmic turning the other cheek. Violence is met with non-violence, and by that act God's acceptance of the world is proved. And another piece of the puzzle is added to our picture.

In fact this study of metaphors for the atonement could go on and on, but I think the point has been made. In the Hebrew Bible one of the defining characteristic of God is steadfast love, that is, the divine commitment to bless humanity and to be bonded to humanity by virtue of God's favor for us. The way God has chosen to do this is not power and force, but by acting in self-sacrificing commitment to us, even when we are at our worst. That is the cross. That is atonement.

If you have met me, then it is likely you have met my dog Lizzie, because she is nearly always with me. She is a beautiful springer spaniel, who embodies all the characteristics of her breed. With a liver and white coat and green eyes, she exemplifies vigor, intelligence, and loyalty. Some time back, I had to leave her with a friend for a weekend. The friend had chores and left my dog alone in her home. Taking advantage of her keeper's absence Lizzie managed to open the back door of the house, go into the back yard, open the latch on the fence, and make her way across Helena. About noon on that Saturday I got a phone call from a staff member who happened to be walking past the diocesan house and found Lizzie sitting at the front door waiting for me to appear. I do not know how she managed to find the office, but I do know she risked her life to be with me.

Magnify that canine loyalty infinitely. Understand that sort of loyalty as part of the heart of God. Then you see the motive behind the cruciform work of atonement.

QUESTIONS FOR DISCUSSION

First, can you think of an incident in your life and in the life of your church when someone has made a sacrifice that brought about reconciliation and healing?

Second, how would you define atonement in your own words?

Third, what image best expresses your idea of atonement?

Fourth, the atonement suggests God in Christ sacrificed all for us. What would you be willing to sacrifice for God in the coming week?

chapter 3

Bible
The B-I-B-L-E, That's the Book for Me

My first Bible came with a fine leather cover and gilt edging. On the cover "Holy Bible" was engraved in gold, and it was printed on fine paper in a nice, crisp print. It was a King James translation with its noble, rolling prose. I am sure it was costly. There was no mistaking that it was an important volume meant to be valued and used for decades.

Some six decades later I still have that Bible, along with many others in various translations and formats. When I work with the Bible I always find it to be holy in the sense that I encounter the presence of the Risen Lord in it, an that in and through the words of the text he is addressing me and the church I serve. That's why I have included the Bible as one of the terms in a basic Christian vocabulary. In this chapter I intend to explore with you three factors about this special book. First, what it is. Second, how it came to be. And third, its role in the life of the baptized.

So, we begin. Briefly, the Bible is a collection of writings; it is the holy book of the church. Other religions have their holy scriptures, and the Bible is ours. The Bible is dominated by stories, by narratives about God encountering God's people, as well as the human response to the saving activity of God. Other genres can be found there, poetry, wisdom literature, letters, etc., but no matter the form the subject is always God and God's mighty deeds on behalf of God's chosen people.

As we glance through its table of contents we note that the Bible consists of a library under one cover. Furthermore, the Bible has several divisions or parts. First is the Old Testament, also called the Hebrew scriptures, covering the history of God's activity from about 1800 BC until 300 BC. This begins with two accounts of the creation of the world followed by the sagas of Abraham, Isaac, and Jacob, the founders of the people of Israel. Then follow the stories of Moses, the judges, the establishment of the united kingdoms of Israel and Judah under David, then the writings of the prophets. Along the way we find the Psalms, wisdom literature, codes and ordinances, and other kinds of literature.

Next, as we glance at the table of contents we find the second major division of the scriptures, the New Testament. This covers the life of Jesus and the beginnings of the church, as well as letters, essays, sermons, and an apocalypse. The time covered takes place from the birth of Jesus and ends at about 120 AD.

At this point we need to take a side step and analyze the term "testament." If you look at older Bibles, particularly the King James Versions, you will see that testament is used as a synonym for covenant. Thus, we could talk about the Old and New Covenant as easily as the Old and New Testament. Underneath these usages lay the understanding that God reached out and established an eternal covenant with the people of Israel; this is the Old Testament story. In Jesus, God reached out and established a covenant with all people; this is the new Testament story. We need to state clearly at this point that the use of "Old Testament" does not suggest that God has ceased to have a covenant with the Jewish people; as Paul reminds us in Romans, the covenants of God are eternal and cannot be revoked.

The idea of covenant or testament requires two parties, because a covenant by definition describes the relationship between two entities. In scripture we discover God's self-description. "The LORD, the LORD, a God merciful and gracious, slow to anger, and abounding in steadfast love and faithfulness, keeping steadfast love for the thousandth generation, forgiving iniquity and transgression and sin." (Exodus 34. 6-7) To put it another way God chooses to deal with the people by means of covenants. The key term is "steadfast love." On the other hand, the people chosen by God are to understand themselves as consecrated to God. That is, their whole lives should be a meditation on living in the presence of such a God. In the New Testament's view that consecrated living is demonstrated by love of God coupled with love of neighbor.

When the first several generations of Christians referred to holy scripture they meant the Old Testament. The writings that would later be collected into the New Testament were still being written, and it would be some centuries later before the church settled on what books to include in the New Testament. The book of 2 Timothy, likely written in the last third of the first century, has this passage: "All scripture is inspired by God and is useful for teaching, for reproof, for correction, and for training in righteousness." (3.16) Here the writer is commenting on the value of reading scripture, in this case, the Old Testament.

This leads us to consider the second point, the history of the development of the Bible. It did not spring fully formed at some point in time, but rather results from a complex process of discernment by the people of God guided by the Spirit. Regarding the Old Testament, for instance, the historian Josephus listed in one of his late first century writings the twenty-four books that are now considered the official Jewish Bible, but his enumeration stands at the end of centuries of development. As noted before those books were shaped in a variety of forms. Some began as oral material, stories and sagas passed by word-of-mouth through many generations and later written down. The book of Judges stands as an example. Other books began in written form, the Psalms being an instance. This material was collected and redacted, and then eventually put together as an assemblage of sacred material. A detailed history of this process has been attempted by many scholars, but I think we need to maintain a humble stance in regard to what we can claim to know about the construction of the Hebrew Bible. After all, it contains two millenia of complicated history involving many people and places of the Middle East.

The book of 2 Kings narrates a fascinating story illustrating a single but important step in the development of the Old Testament. You can find it in chapters twenty-two and twenty-three. The protagonist of the story is Josiah (640-609 BC), King of Judah. He was considered the best king to rule in Jerusalem excepting only the great David. Josiah decided to repair the Temple, seen as the dwelling place of God on earth. During the construction a scroll was discovered, read by the high priest, who rushed to share it with Josiah. What stuns us is that this was a book of the law, apparently tucked away and forgotten. Likely it represented an early form of the book of Deuteronomy. Can you imagine simply losing part of the Bible? The book was read to King Josiah, who tore his clothes in that traditional act of grief. He says that the ancestors of his people had disobeyed God, and the whole of Judah was now in danger of the God's judgment because of this disobedience. Not sure what to do he consulted the prophetess Huldah, who confirmed his worst suspicions, that God intended to bring disaster on the people because of their sins.

Josiah takes decisive action, hoping to divert judgment. He has the book read to all the people. He has all the temples of Baal and Asherah, the foreign gods of fertility, destroyed, and all signs of pagan worship are dismantled. A secondary temple of God had been built in Bethel, and Josiah destroyed it, thus focusing all worship in Judah on the temple in Jerusalem. He cast out all wizards and mediums. But maybe most significantly he reinstituted the celebration of Passover, which had not been celebrated since the days of the judges centuries before.

By these actions Josiah elevated the stature of the book of Deuteronomy. By royal mandate it became part of the official life of the God's people, and it remains so to this day.

The story of the New Testament's development is simpler because it embraces a much shorter time period, from the early 50's till about 110 or 120. The earliest part of the New Testament to be valued as holy scripture were certain writings by St. Paul. The gospel of John may be the last of the New Testament works to be written. In 369 St. Athanasius wrote a letter in which he for the first time listed what we today consider the New Testament.

The church seemed to have used three criteria for their selection of New Testament books. First, was it apostolic? Did an apostle and someone close to an apostle author the work? We can call this the test of apostolicity. Second, was it being used by most of the church? That is, did Christians sense in these writing a word from God, and did others have that same experience? We can call this the test of catholicity. And third, did the teaching in the book adhere to the proclamation of the apostles? We can call this the test of orthodoxy. By these standards the church judged which writings were to function as authoritative scripture in the life of the church.

The Bibles used by Roman Catholics, the Orthodox, and Anglicans contain a third selection of books called the apocrypha or the deuterocanonicals. They represent a sort of "junior varsity" collection. They are used by Roman Catholics and the Orthodox for doctrinal purposes, but are not considered as important as the Old and New Testaments; Anglicans use them for devotional purposes only. The apocrypha developed between the third century BC till the first century AD. During this period Jewish scholars began the work of translating their scriptures from Hebrew into Greek, the common language of the day. They worked on all the books we know as the Old Testament plus fifteen other works by Jewish writers. This great accomplishment is called the Septuagint, abbreviated as LXX. Later, St. Jerome (347-420 AD) translated the Bible into the then common language of the day, Latin. His work, known as the Vulgate, became the standard translation in the Latin-speaking world. His translation included the apocrypha.

We should stop at this point and summarize key points. First, the church chose the contents of holy scripture. This fact, if forgotten, opens the door to an unhealthy fundamentalism. Second, the selection process involved what books Christians were actually used in worship, preaching, and catechism. They chose what seemed to them to be holy, a word from God for their situation. Third, there was a winnowing process that occurred. Not every gospel written was included in their selections. Recently a flurry of articles and books have suggested that the church has hidden away gospels that seem to question the four canonical gospels. No such thing happened. Any seminary library has copies of these ancient writings, but what is overlooked is that the church did not find them worthy of inclusion in the collection of holy writings. Four, the official list of books in the Christian Bible, called the canon of scripture, was not settled until the fourth century. By this time the church liturgy had developed, the ordered ministry of the church was set, and the creeds had been fixed. This should not distract from our sense of the importance of Bible, but rather, should stand as a testimony to the value of the Bible.

When we participate in the Holy Eucharist, one of the major components of that event is the solemn reading of scripture. The common response to the first two lessons is for the lector to say at the conclusion of the reading "The Word of the Lord." To that the congregations replies "Thanks be to God.

This little dialogue between reader and people elicits the question of the authority of the Bible in the life of the church, our third point. We can find many possible ways to respond to that issues, but the little liturgical dialogue noted above offers a fruitful way to proceed.

Jesus is the primary word of God. The soaring opening chapter of John's gospel says it perfectly: "And the Word became flesh and lived among us, and we have seen his glory, the glory as of a father's only son, full of grace and truth." (1.14) "Word" here stands as a translation of the Greek term *Logos*. It suggests the logic of God's mind, how God thinks, what God wants to say. Jesus is exactly that.

Scripture is the word of God in a secondary sense. Christians have always said that scripture---all of it---points to Jesus, and that we read the scripture in light of the incarnation, ministry, death, and resurrection of Christ. So, the read scripture pulls us closer to the one who is the Word of God.

But a third layer of meanings also occurs. Any preaching or teaching of the scripture can be the word of God, too. Who has not experienced a sermon or read a book based on the Bible which seems to be a means of God addressing them?

The authority of scripture, then, is based on the experience of the Risen Lord. In and through the Bible he addresses us with compelling words of both comfort and challenge. Because of this, we assent to and recognize the ability of the Bible to be a dependable medium of God's presence and communication. Therein lies its authority.

But just here we enter dangerous ground. Some want to connect the authority of the Bible with the concept of inspiration. They claim that the writers of the Bible were like secretaries taking dictation from God. It follows, then, that every word of scripture is perfect and without contradiction or error. This idea encapsulates a key ingredient in fundamentalism.

But grave issues accompany this. For instance, this view violates human freedom and intelligence. That is, can we say that God overrode the minds and wills of biblical writers in order to dictate the scriptures? I think not. This view also fails to recognize the variety of points of view in the Bible. Many psalms, for instance, cry out to God to punish one's enemies, even to the point of asking for death for the opponents. That clearly does not jibe with Jesus' command to love our enemies. Finally, the fundamentalist approach tends to overlook the historical nature of the Bible. We need to recall, for example, that some of the calls for violent bloodshed in the Old Testament reflect Bronze Age tribal mentality, and that God's people grew over time in their understanding of God's nature and will.

Allow me an instance of inspiration in the biblical sense. As I preach I certainly hope that my sermons are inspired. I want what I say to be Jesus' word to at least some of those present. With that hope in mind, I prepare my sermons with study, with prayer, and with careful consideration. But I never have had the sense that God was dictating word-by-word what I should say. I do trust that the presence of the Risen Christ will be at work in my mind, will, and heart, and that he will speak to me through the holy writings of the Bible. That, for me, is inspiration. And I am bold to say that I believe the writers and redactors of scripture worked in a similar way.

Let's conclude with a Bible story that pulls together what we have considered together. Here it is:

> Now an angel of the Lord said to Philip, "Get up and go toward the south to that road that goes down from Jerusalem to Gaza." (This is the wilderness road.) So he got up and went. Now there was an Ethiopian eunuch, a court official of the Candace, queen of the Ethiopians, in charge of her entire treasury. He had come to Jerusalem to worship, and was returning home; seated in his chariot, he was reading the prophet Isaiah. Then the Spirit spoke to Philip, "Go over to this chariot and join it." So Philip ran up to it and heard him reading the prophet Isaiah. He asked, "Do you understand what you are reading?" He replied, "How can I, unless someone guides me?" And he invited Philip to get in and sit beside him. Now the passage of the scripture that he was reading was this: "Like a sheep he was led to the slaughter, and like a lamb silent before its shearers, so he does not open his mouth. In his humiliation justice was denied him. Who can describe his generation? For his life is taken away from the earth." The eunuch asked Philip, "About whom, may I ask you, does the prophet say this, about himself or about someone else?" Then Philip began to speak, and starting with the scripture, he proclaimed to him the good news about Jesus. As they were going along the road, they came to some water; and the eunuch said, "Look, here is water! What is to prevent me from being baptized?" He commanded the chariot to stop, and both of them, Philip and the eunuch went down into the water, and Philip baptized him. (Acts 8.26-38)

We have met Philip earlier in chapter nine of Acts; he was one of the seven men ordained deacon in order to care for the Greek-speaking widows in the church. His name indicates a Greek background. The eunuch is a high royal official, and the facts that he has a chariot, owns a book, and can travel the long journey to Jerusalem indicate education, wealth and power. The eunuch is reading a key passage from Isaiah (53. 7-8), which is part of a series of poems scholars refer to as "servant songs." The basic idea is that God will raise up an obedient servant who will accomplish God's will through humility and suffering. Isaiah had in mind the people of Israel as the suffering servant, but Philip sees the prophecy by the light of the death and resurrection of Jesus. Philip takes on the role of teacher and interpreter, and the result is the eunuch being baptized into the death and resurrection of Christ.

In this fascinating and dramatic passage of holy scripture, a section of the Hebrew Bible functions as the means by which the Word of God spoke to the eunuch. The scriptural word, interpreted by a teacher through the lens of Jesus' cross and resurrection, led to a saving and life-changing encounter with the Word himself. This is the way the Bible works in Christs' church, then and now.

When I was growing up church people were still expected to memorize verses from the Bible. In fact, my grandmother would pay me a dime for every verse I committed to memory. A half century later those verses are still there, rattling around in my mind, and rising to consciousness just when I need them. Those verses inhabit me soul. Again and again, Jesus has used them to speak to me at the points of my need. The Bible has been central to my life. I always meet Jesus there. And that is my testimony to the authority of scripture.

DISCUSSION QUESTIONS

First, do you have a Bible story or verse that has helped shape your life?

Second, taking account of where you stand in your now, what new verse or Bible story might be a means of being encountered by Christ?

Three, do you have a discipline about reading the Bible? If not, consider developing a realistic plan to work with the Bible daily.

Four, when was the last time the Bible opened new doors or broke down barriers in your life?

Five, what Bible story does your church most need to hear?

chapter 4

Catholic
The Whole Thing

HERE ARE TWO STATEMENTS. I'm Catholic. I'm catholic. Did you catch the distinction? It is an important one. The word "Catholic" refers to the Roman Catholic Church. Instead of saying "I am Roman Catholic" most people simply drop the "Roman" from their comment. The word "catholic" describes a certain quality or attribute of the church. In the Nicene Creed, four marks of the church mentioned: one, holy, catholic, and apostolic. Most churches want to claim all four characteristics, and the particular church headquartered in Rome seeks to make a special claim to one of the marks. In this chapter I will seek to explain one of the richest and most important terms in the Christian vocabulary.

St. Ignatius of Antioch first ascribed the term "catholic" to the church, and this happened as early as 112 AD. In his day, the four great urban areas which had churches, Jerusalem, Antioch, Alexandria, and Rome, were called "catholic" by Ignatius. This served as a method of rooting the faith in important cities. Part of being catholic was to be able to connect with the beginning of the church. Jerusalem, Antioch, and Rome could all claim to have been founded by an apostle, and Alexandria said that the evangelist Mark had established their church. Rootedness, then, is part of being a catholic church.

In the fourth and fifth centuries the church was subjected to persecution under the Roman emperor Diocletian. During that time some of the leaders of the church, including bishops and priests, renounced their faith in order to escape the harsh hand of the empire. As the persecution ended, these people were called" the lapsed", but, despite that, they wanted to return to the Christian fold. In the literature of the time those who remained faithful were termed "catholic" as opposed to the lapsed. As a side note, this was called the Donatist Controversy, some wanting to expel the lapsed and some wishing to allow their return. It was St. Augustine of Hippo who stated the case that won the day. His basic idea was that the sacraments of the church did not depend on the holiness or faithfulness of the officiants. Thus, the lapsed were able to rejoin the church.

In the fifth century Vincent of Levin stated what has become a definition of a catholic church. According to Vincent a catholic church advocates the faith believed everywhere, always, and at all times. The problem is that it would be hard to identify a church that consistently meets that standard. Nevertheless, this definition continues to be used, especially in polemical ways over against supposedly inadequate churches.

So far we can state, then, that a catholic church has ancient roots and is ready to defend correct doctrine and worship.

Today, if you were to do a person-on-the-street interview you would probably hear that "catholic" means universal and general as opposed to local and denominational. But I hope you sense that lacks depth and an understanding of the history of the word.

Let me offer what I hope will be a more positive and less polemical understanding of the term. First, catholic comes from a Greek word that means literally "according to the whole." It connotes fullness, wholeness, completion. Imagine a basket filled to overflowing with ripe, colorful fruits and vegetables. That is the sense of the world.

Then, apply that understanding not just to doctrine but also to worship, piety, and the life of the church. Understand that "catholic" addresses the whole life of the Christian community.

So, the opposite of 'catholic' would be sectarian, narrow, eccentric, and tribal. That word "sect" denotes something important. A sect would have characteristics that were not rooted, not part of the great basket of the church. For instance, think of a community that denies the Trinity, or that finds the Nicene Creed highly problematic. That would be a sect, a community that is not catholic.

But here is the bottom line. The good news of Jesus Christ is big enough to include all people at all times and in all places. Catholicity, then, stands at the very heart of the gospel. In so far as any church functioning with this understanding, we can see the key sense of "catholic" at work. And this quickly spreads to other matters.

As an example, allow me to use my own Episcopal Church as an instance. We see ourselves as a fully catholic church. And we point to four factors that we believe describe a catholic church. We see the Nicene and Apostles Creed as sufficient, accurate and ancient definitions of belief. We hold up the two gospel sacraments of Baptism and Eucharist as means of grace and necessary for salvation. We believe the Old and New Testaments to be the written word of God. And we state that the church ordered according to the historic episcopate with bishops being successors of the apostles. You may or may not agree, but it is our way helping celebrate the catholic gospel of Jesus.

To close, we look at a crucial incident in the life of the first generation of the church. Acts 15 records the event, and St. Paul, one of the principle players in the story, gives his account in Galatians 2. The earliest Christians were, like Jesus himself, Jewish. At that time Jews were especially concerned about maintaining their identity as a people, and part of the way they did that was to state that the world was composed of two kinds of people, Jews and non-Jews, whom they called Gentiles. Jews did not normally have any close associations with Gentiles. Because they had been given the Law and had an eternal covenant with God they rightly saw themselves as special and unique, and, therefore, they had to fence themselves off from the influences of the largely Gentile world. Then along comes Jesus followed by the evangelical work of early Christians. As a result some Gentiles were seeking baptism and wanted to be part of the church. But for the Jewish Christians this presented a huge obstacle. They put it in stark terms: unless you became a Jew you could not be saved.

The apostles and elders of the church met in Jerusalem to adjudicate this issue. Presiding at the meeting was no less a person than Jesus' own brother James. Peter spoke first, advocating the inclusion of Gentiles. He said in part, "God, who knows the human heart, testified to them by giving them the Holy Spirit, just as he did to us . . . Now, therefore, why are you putting God to the test by placing on the neck of the disciples a yoke that either our ancestors not we have been able to bear. On the contrary, we believe we will be saved through the grace of the Lord Jesus." (Acts 15. 9-11). Remember that Peter was himself Jewish and had earlier in his life refused even to eat with Gentiles. Then Paul and Barnabas, both Jews, step forward and witness to all the signs and wonders God had done among the Gentiles.

The council closes with a decree from James. He notes that the conversion of Gentiles accords with the Old Testament, and says, "Therefore, I have reached the decision that we should not trouble those Gentiles who are turning to God." (15. 19)

In that step the church became catholic. And I, a Gentile, am most happy about that! The mercy of God is now understood to extend to the whole world.

But this story has a cutting edge for us today if we are to maintain our claim to be catholic Christians. Is Jesus big enough for our enemies, those people whom we despise, who ignite anger and resentment in us? Is Jesus big enough for those whom we see as simply beyond the pale? Is Jesus big enough for people who disgust us or who call everything we value into question? To be catholic is not a call to practice mere tolerance. We are called to love in the same way that Jesus loves us, without condition and without barriers. Are we catholic enough to be part of the one, holy, catholic, and apostolic church?

DISCUSSION QUESTIONS

First, before reading this chapter how would you have defined the word "catholic"?

Second, who or what makes it difficult for you to practice being a catholic?

Third, in Matthew 2 we hear the story of Magi visiting the infant Jesus. These were likely astrologers from Persia and would have been considered pagan foreigners. What are some of the catholic implications of that story?

Four, what does your church need to do to open its doors wider?

chapter 5

Church

You Can't Be a Christian Alone

LET ME BEGIN WITH three stories. When I was a teen, my father took my sister and me aside, and made this declaration, "I don't care how late you are out on Saturday night, you are going to church on Sunday morning." That communicated to me his commitment to Christ and the church, and indicated how important it was to him.

When we went to church over one entrance was carved "Domus Dei" and over another "Porta Coeli." I had had enough Latin to know the translation: House of God, Gate of Heaven. This harkens back to the story of Jacob's dream at Bethel (Genesis 28. 10-19), in which he is encountered by God. When he wakes the next morning, he exclaims, "How awesome is this place! This is none other than the house of God and this is the gate of heaven." (28.17) And while I have had nothing like the dramatic experience of Jacob, I sensed that those phrases accurately described what took place in this sacred place.

Many years later I took part in a class in which we learned the importance of knowing and being able to share our God story, the occasions when we could sense God acting in our lives. As part of our instruction each of us spent time with some lay people from the local community. From that I learned something that surprised me: people generally cannot separate their story of God from the story of their church.

We can all tell both sad and funny stories about church people. But beneath that lies some important truths. We cannot be Christians alone.

The church community shapes our relationship with God and with each other in important ways. And among the last things the Risen Lord did before his departure from this world was to found the church. Church is important, very important.

Our word "church" has an Old English origin, and means "of the Lord." So we must tie together the human community with the Risen Lord; that, at least, is the implication of this etymology. In English translations of the New Testament, the term "church" denotes the Greek word *ekklesia*. In the most literal sense it means, "those called out" or "those chosen." Thus, the writer of the New Testament book of 1 Peter can address Christians in this way: "You are a chosen race, a royal priesthood, a holy nation, God's own people." (2. 9) That is the church!

St. Paul enables us to deepen our definition of the church in 1 Corinthians 12. He is dealing with the issue of rather severe divisions in the church in the city of Corinth, and he offers an image to help them envision themselves in a wholesome way. He asks them to imagine the church as a human body. It has many parts, eyes, ears, hands, feet, but it remains one body. Moreover, the body has one head, one brain, which controls it. The members have different roles and capabilities, but still are intimately connected. Then Paul delivers the punch line, "Now you are the Body of Christ and individually members of it." (12. 27) Earlier he tells the Corinthians are initiated into the body of Christ: "For in the one Spirit we were all baptized into one body---Jews or Greeks, slaves or free---and were all made to drink of one Spirit." (12: 13) That is, baptism makes us part of the body of Christ, and that reality is sustained in the Eucharist.

We can summarize this scriptural passage with three statements. All the baptized are united together as members of the one Body, Christ's church. All the baptized have a proper role to play in the work of the Body. Finally, it is all about Jesus, the head of the Body.

We now must face two issues, both of which represent common positions in our culture. The first will sound familiar. The church is just a collection of hypocrites. This rather scornful position allows many to denigrate the value of the church and its ministry. The sarcastic response says, "Yes, of course, and there is plenty of room for you." Not helpful! But it does suggest that we must admit that no one lives with perfect integrity. No one functions with singleness of heart. The church, however, reamins a favorite target.

In high school I was part of the marching band, and we took part in four or five major parades each year. My position was usually on the left side of the front row, a place that allowed me to hear all the comments of the bystanders. Some of those people enjoyed saying, "Oh, look! That person is out of step." It angered me. If you have been part of a marching unit you know that everyone gets out of step occasionally. Furthermore, it takes no special skill to spot that unfortunate person; it is perfectly clear who has made a misstep. In the church everyone sins, and usually people know it. But the larger truth remains that most church members participate regularly, are serious about it, and do pretty well most of the time. Maybe all of this should remind the church that our society expects great things from the Christian community.

The second issue usually comes out this way. The church is a place where I come to be inspired. I want to be feed and made to feel better. Sound familiar, even among church members?

First, I need to say the church is a people, not a building or place. The building is there is to enable the worship and work of the people.

And then I hope you recognize that this comment reveals an astonishing level of individualism and self-interest. It seems to say: the church exists for me. These statements always call to my mind the image of the church as a spiritual cafeteria. I walk through and pick this and that, eat, and then go my own way. Social commentators have noted frequently that we live in a culture that is individualistic in unprecedented ways. We have become so focused on the individual, his needs, her desires, his rights, her demands, that we find ourselves confused, even paralyzed. For example, we are continually involved in controversies about one person's right to speak his or her mind, even when it damages the rights or reputation of others. It is always about "me."

But the church is an altogether different entity. The church's work consists of constantly pointing to Jesus Christ. Our testimony states that only he cannot fulfill our deepest needs and empower us to live life to the full. We always stand in need of more of Jesus, more of his mercy, more of his presence, more of his grace.

Then we should quickly add that the church is the community in which people can be encountered by the living Lord. This happens primarily through the proclamation of the Word, the administration of the sacraments, prayer, study, service to the community beyond the church, and through the words and actions of the people of the church. You sense, I hope, that we focus outward, toward Jesus, toward others, toward the needy and outcast.

And we do all of this together. The church is always about the community of Christ. We cannot baptize ourselves. We cannot celebrate the Eucharist alone. We cannot read the Bible accurately by ourselves. We are in the Christ business together. We rejoice together. We mourn together. We care for each other. We support each other. I personally believe that our society today longs for significant community. We need more than people we "hang out" with. We need the community where we are known, cared for, and involved in big and important work. We need the church.

I recently had a conversation with a deeply spiritual and committed member of her church. She has the right vision of what the church can be. But she said, "If I had trouble there is no one in this church that I could call." Sad, indeed. She knew painfully well that her congregation was not living into being the church. What about your church?

But we do well sometimes. One of the great privileges of my life is administering the consecrated bread and cup at communion. I believe that I am giving people the Body and Blood of Christ, that they are communing with the Risen Lord actually present in bread and wine. And I know what is happening in the lives of at least some of the people. That man is afraid of losing his job. She has no friends at school. That couple has a bad marriage. And they come to the altar with empty and open hands and hearts. You can see it sometimes in their eyes. They want Jesus. They need his presence and mercy. And at the altar, at the crossroad of this world and the next, Jesus welcomes them and gives them life.

DISCUSSION QUESTIONS

First, make a list of words that describes your church. What insights do you have? What are you going to do about it?

Two, what talents, skills, and experiences can you offer to the life of the Body of Christ?

Three, we must deal with the duality of the church as community and the church as a building. How can you make a proper balance for your life as an individual and as a member of the church?

Four, how can we help people celebrate baptism as initiation into the Body of Christ?

chapter 6

Cross
Love, Not Power

If you visit Rome you may want to seek out the ancient church of Santa Sabina. As you enter notice the huge wooden doors, and then look at the upper left panel on the right-hand door. There you will spot a rather crudely done carving of Christ on the cross. This church dates from the fifth century, and the little carving probably represents the oldest known portrayal of the cross.

Scholars suggest that Jesus died in about 28 AD, but it took the church four hundred years to make a representation of this central episode in salvation history. That fact indicates how hard it was for the early generations of Christians to deal with the cross. No one denied that Jesus had died in that manner, but they did not want to go so far as to picture of it.

Their reluctance, I suspect, was based in the reality of crucifixion. The Roman government reserved it for runaway slaves, highway robbers, and people guilty of treason, all of which were considered especially heinous crimes by the empire. It was so horrible that it was used only with non-Romans. The crucifixion involved loss of blood, shock ensued, and the victim usually died of asphyxiation. It could go on for days before death came. Our American constitution protects us from cruel and unusual punishment, but the very point of Roman crucifixion was that it was cruel and unusual. It warned people of the dire consequences of thwarting the rule of the empire.

Today we see the cross everywhere, it serves as the central symbol of our faith, and it calls us to focus on Jesus. For the early church it seemed horrible almost beyond words or pictures. The analogue for us would be to erect symbolic electric chairs as a sign of faith.

The accounts of Jesus' crucifixion in the gospels are written without sentimentality or sensationalism, and can be characterized as laconic. They stand as instances of "just the facts." Yet along with resurrection accounts the crucifixion stories function as the climax of Jesus' life and ministry.

In the rest of the New Testament two factors dominate the discussion about the cross. One is the suffering of Jesus on the cross. The book of Hebrews, for instance, has a great deal to say about the meaning and significance of the cross, but it highlights Jesus' suffering as a key factor in the cross. Consider this passage: "We do see Jesus, who for a little while was made lower than the angels, not crowned with glory and honor because of the suffering of death, so that by the grace of God he might taste death for everyone." (2. 9) Part of the message of the crucifixion is that God in Christ has drunk deeply from the chalice of human pain, suffering, and death. And there, paradoxically, lies the glory of Christ. His willingness to participate in the fullness of human life signals his commitment to and solidarity with us. God has trod the valley of the shadow of death as an act of steadfastness and faithfulness to humanity.

Like it or not, suffering defines Jesus' and God's mission.

Beside suffering shame plays a major part in the New Testament understanding of Jesus. This finds its basis in a part of Jewish law that may not be easily comprehensible to us. Here is the pertinent passage from Deuteronomy: "When someone is convicted of a crime punishable by death and is executed, and you hang him on a tree, his corpse must not remain all night upon the tree; you shall bury him that same day, for anyone hung on a tree is under God's curse. You must not defile the land that the LORD your God is giving you for possession." (21.22-23) Certainly part of the shame lies in the public nature of the criminal's death. It is one thing to know that capital punishment was carried out, but it quite another to see the person on public display with his face clearly visible.

But something more is at work here. Note that the dead body defiles the land. The best analogy I know is that they saw this in almost bacterial terms. The evil of the man and the curse of God could pass to the land in the way cold germs pass from one person to another. Not only was the victim a criminal, but God cursed that person, and the evil and curse could infect the land and pollute it. If not dealt with this evil might show itself in terms of bad crops, sickness, and tragic turns of events for those who lived on the land.

When I go to my favorite hamburger place I see on the menu that I can get a sandwich with a single patty, two patties, or even three patties. I suppose the idea is that if one is delicious, then two or three will be double or triple delicious. The shame of the cross is a triple helping, shame on shame on shame.

And that, too, represents part of the crucifixion message. Where is God to be found? If you accept the story of the cross, you can find good beyond the boundaries of what is proper and good, even in the hell and nightmare we create for ourselves. Shame is declawed, rendered powerless, because of the lovingkindness of God.

So, we can confidently say that the cross and the issues it poses for us have been central to Christian thought and discussion from New Testament times forward. Even today it stands at the heart of a controversy about the nature of the gospel. The argument focuses on the theory of substitutionary atonement. This position states that someone had to pay for the sins of the world in order for God's holiness and justice to be appeased. Thus, Jesus' death was the price paid to God for human sin and rebellion. This represents a standard position for some in the church, but you may well already sense the problem. This view makes Jesus into God's divine whipping boy, and it portrays God as something close to a moral monster in demanding the death of his son. I have tried to tackle this in two previous books (*Living the Resurrection: Reflections after Easter*, and *Journey with Jesus: Encountering Christ in his Birth, Baptism, Death, and Resurrection*), and you can refer to the article on Atonement in this book.

I ardently do not believe that the New Testament teaches substitutionary atonement. I see other, more helpful ways of understanding the cross. One states that the cross stands as both the sign and the means of imparting of God's love. I know no more powerful statement of this than the gospel of John's introduction to the last days of Jesus' life. "Now before the festival of the Passover, Jesus knew that his hour had come to depart from this world and go to the Father. Having loved his own who were in the world, he loved them to the end." (13:1-2) Love in scripture is not an emotion or feeling. It is, rather, steadfast commitment to another, even to the point of sacrifice. And in this verse the phrase "to the end" contains a key idea. The Greek term used is *teleos*, which connotes fulfilment and completion. It is not an issue of time, as in "The bell has rung, and class is at an end." Rather, it suggests completion of a task. Furthermore, in scripture it also suggests something completed according the God's plan. So the sense of the verse is that Jesus loved his disciples according to God's plan, to the fulfillment of God's will, perfectly, and fully. This, of course, means the cross, which signals and conveys perfect, divine love, the complete commitment of God to humanity.

Thus, when we look at Jesus hanging on the tree, we see an instance of everything that could have gone wrong actually happening. We see human rejection of all that is good, true, and beautiful. And yet, Jesus embraced it and made it his own. On the cross he broke the cycle of vengeance, violence and judgment, and that includes any of our ideas about divine vengeance on human sin. On the cross God embraces humanity even at its worst. This divine love touches the deepest part of human need.

Here is how one prayer states it: "Lord Jesus Christ, you stretched out your arms of love on the hard wood of the cross that everyone might come within the reach of your saving embrace." (The Book of Common Prayer, p. 101)

The cross, furthermore, stands as God's response to the problem of pain. You know the problem and may have said it yourself. If God is loving and powerful, why does God allow pain and suffering to persist? I have never been able to find a clear, simple, twenty-five-words-or-less answer, and perhaps there is none. But I do understand the cross to be God's response to this agonizing issue. The cross says that as we endure the tragedies and pains of life, God knows, God cares, and God shares intimately in them. And if we link the cross with the resurrection, we sense God's promise that God loves us to the end, and that in the end, all will be made well.

I recently notified the seminarians from my diocese that I had registered them to take the dreaded General Ordination Exam. In The Episcopal Church candidates for ordination are required to take an extensive exam as part of the way the bishop evaluates those candidates readiness to be ordained. The exam generates enormous amounts of anguish and anxiety. Within hours of my e-mail I received responses. I am really nervous about this. I am not sure I can pass. What are the details? Even though it has been long ago I, too, took an ordination exam. I know what it is like, because I sat for days at a time in front of a typewriter answering questions. I also know these seminarians. I explained some of the workings of the test. I told them that they would do better than they expected, and that I knew they would pass. It's a small instance, I know, but on the grand scale of God's providence it works the same way. From the cross, God can say, I know. I care. And finally, all will be well.

DISCUSSION QUESTIONS

First, do you wear a cross or display a cross in your home or office? If so, why?

Two, write a short letter to Jesus, thanking him for what he did on the cross. What would you say to him?

Three, explain the meaning of the cross for you.

Four, Google "pictures of the crucifixion" and then chose the one that touches you most.

chapter 7

Doctrine and Dogma
Teaching and Learning

IF SOMEONE WERE TO say to me, "You are such a dogmatic person," I would likely feel angry. If another person then chimed in and said, "Yes, indeed. You are so doctrinaire," I would become furious. We avoid the terms "doctrine" and "dogma" because they hang heavy with negative connotations. They suggest a person with a rigid turn of mind and someone with too much confidence in his or her own point of view. Most us want to perceive ourselves are flexible and humble, not rigid and haughty. We, therefore, avoid those two terms at all costs.

Because of that attitude, we need clarity about our understanding of doctrine and dogma. They occur commonly in the conversation of Christian people, and in that context they carry no emotional weight or sense of condemnation. As with many English words, we should look to Latin to find the seed from which our word grows. *Docere* simply means to teach, and in that language carries connotations of being honorable and worthy. Doctrine, then, refers to the teaching of the church. The Apostle's Creed, for example, can act as an instance of doctrine.

Dogma stands as a more formal matter. In general, it denotes a decree by an authority. Rooted in Greek, it points to something we believe to be true. It is dogma for Americans that we have the right to free speech; that has been officially stated in no less an authority than the Bill of Rights. In church usage dogma tends to refer to an important teaching that the church holds to be basic and important. For Episcopalians we could call the Nicene Creed an instance of dogma.

We can see doctrine at work in the New Testament itself. Colossians, likely written sometime after 65, quotes an early Christians hymn. And, as is the case with many hymns, it states doctrine in poetic form.

> "[Jesus] is the image of the invisible God, the firstborn of all creation; for in him all things in heaven and on earth were created, things visible and invisible, whether thrones or dominions or rulers or powers---all things have been created through him and for him. He himself is before all things and in him all things hold together. He is the head of the body, the church; he is the beginning, the firstborn from the dead, so that he might come to have first place in everything. For in him all the fullness of God was pleased to dwell, and through him God was pleased to reconcile himself to all things, whether on earth or in heaven, by making peace through the blood of the cross." (1: 15-20)

You can sense that the writer is spinning out the implications of Jesus' death and resurrection. You can perceive, I hope, the writer saying, "Jesus, God in the flesh, died and was raised. Therefore, it must follow that he is the first of everything, and is the head of the church, and that all of God was pleased to dwell in him and to do carry out God's reconciling work." That is the way doctrine works. I suspect most Christians do some doctrinal thinking from time to time.

Compare this passage with one from 1 John. "Who is the liar but the one who denies that Jesus was the Christ? This is the antichrist, the who denies the Father and the Son. No one who denies the Son has the Father; everyone who confesses the Son has the Father also." (2: 22-23) The writer is addressing a errant teaching called Docetism, which threatened the early church. Docetism said that Jesus only seemed to be divine but was not fully the embodiment of God. You sense the determined and insistent tone of the passage. Note also that it draws a line: on one side stands a lying antichrist, and on the other is the faithful Christian. Here we have dogma at work. In the face of opposition and misunderstanding the apostolic writer states doctrine and then insists on its truth.

Lest we become judgmental about dogma, understand that we use dogma today. Most people, for instance, believe that children should be vaccinated against small pox, pertussis, measles, etc. In the face of people who do not hold that believe, the majority rises up, cites science, and insists that all little kids should have their shots. And they sometimes are able to enforce that by school or health department regulations.

A common part of congregational life is confirmation. Young people spend a period of time studying the basics of the faith, and then in a public event and in the presence of their chief pastor, the bishop, they affirm their baptismal faith and from the bishop receive the laying on of hands as the means of receiving God's strengthening presence. The pre-confirmation training traditionally takes place by using a catechism, which explains basic doctrine in a question-and-answer form. For example, here is a tidbit from the catechism of The Episcopal Church. Question: What is the Trinity? Answer: The Trinity is one God: Father, Son, and Holy Spirit. (Book of Common Prayer, p. 852) This catechetical approach as preparation for a person affirming his or her baptism sets out a good instance of the role of doctrine in the church.

Some people object to doctrine and dogma on the grounds that it seems to interfere with their personal belief system. Besides the fact that being a Christian is not simply a private and personal affair (see the article above on church), we should not be surprised that Christians have official teaching. Visit the dental hygienist and you will learn the doctrine about the need for and the proper way of brushing your teeth. Go to a baseball game and you will soon learn that that game cannot proceed without the official Rules of Baseball. The church, too, quite naturally has and needs official teaching.

Some years back my family and I visited the Canaan Valley State Park in beautiful West Virginia. We spend part of nearly every day doing some hiking. The trails there are delineated by a series of blazes. These are white stripes painted on trees. You simply follow the blazes to make your journey through the park. Part of the value of doctrine and dogma rests in its usefulness in guiding us on our pilgrimage through life with Jesus. They help us know Jesus, how to recognize his presence, where to meet him, and how to live with meaning and hope.

Christianity consists of a living relationship with Jesus Christ, crucified and risen. Baptism initiates and seals that relationship, which is nurtured by scripture, Eucharist, and prayer. The heart of our faith rests on an abiding communion with Jesus. Inevitably we need to think about that, to grapple with the issues it raises, and work out how we worship and serve Jesus. That is where doctrine and dogma come into play. Doctrine results from reasoned reflection on our life with our Lord.

Some fifteen years ago I decided that I needed a dog. The paper advertised a large litter of English springer spaniels for sale. When I went to visit the kennel the dogs poured forth from their pen, and one little pup ran up to me and jumped into my arms. Thus began my relationship with Lizzie. She is with me nearly all the time and accompanies me everywhere, including churches. We have a relationship. Over the years I have learned a thing or two about dogs. In fact, I have some dog dogma. For example, you have to talk and sing to your dog often. You have to give your dog undivided attention for at least twenty minutes a day. You absolutely cannot ever under any circumstances physically hurt your dog. That states my reasoned reflection about living with Lizzie.

If this is true with dogs, imagine how much we need reasoned reflection about God.

DISCUSSION QUESTIONS

First, think about your experience with Jesus. Can you make two or three assertions about that, which you believe to be true?

Second, of all the doctrines set forth in the Nicene Creed, which are most important for you?

Three, does your church offer ways for you to think theologically, to work on the doctrine of the church?

Four, what doctrine troubles you most? Why?

chapter 8

Faith
What Do I Trust?

WHEN I WAS IN junior high school I played some football. I was always assigned to the line. Now I have never had much athletic ability, but it was fun to play as long as no one expected me to catch the ball. We were always instructed, "Hold the line. Stand firm."

Those instructions suggest the original sense of faith in both languages of the Bible, Hebrew and Greek. The word "faith" means to be steady, to continue in place, to hold the line.

My job requires that I drive all over the geographically huge state of Montana. As I do that I cross over many bridges, and I do so with hardly a thought or worry about it. I am confident that the bridge can carry me and in my SUV safely over the river.

That represents the second sense of faith. To have faith is to live with trust, to be able to put confidence in someone or something. In fact, in the New Testament it connotes complete trust and utter confidence.

So we have two nuances for the word "faith." Jesus manages to pull both together in his teaching. Let's consider the parable of the house built on rock in Matthew's gospel. "Everyone then who hears these words of mine and acts on them will be like a wise man who built his house on rock. The rain fell, the flood came, and the winds blew and beat on that house, but it did not fall, because it had been founded on rock. And everyone who hears these words of mine and does not act on them will be like a foolish man who built his house of and. The rain fell, the floods came, the winds blew and beat against that house, and it fell---and great was its fall." (7: 24-27) Simply hearing Jesus' teachings is not enough; you also have to act on them, to live them out. That is, you have to have faith in Jesus to the point where you shape your life on the basis of his words. The parable also has a sharp side that we need to acknowledge. Faith placed in a wrong or false place can lead to the collapse of one's life.

I love to listen to old-time radio when I drive my truck. Several of those dramas state that they want their stories to show what they believed was a truth: crime does not pay. And the story line always unfolds according to that belief; the bad guys are found out and punished. To put it in the imagery of the parable, the criminals were foolish and had pursued a life that would end in disaster, namely, jail.

In the parable Jesus invites us to trust him, to place our faith in him, to stand fast in what he offers. And if we do that the parable implies a promise about our future: you will find Jesus to be trustworthy, ready and able to support you. If Jesus is trustworthy, then trust him. This would be a wise and solid way to live.

The constant call of scripture consists of the challenge to live our lives on the basis that God is both good and steadfast. And Jesus serves as the case study for that claim.

But faith does not come easily for some people, including me. After all we cannot see God, nor can we test and measure God in the way that a scientist evaluates experiments. In college I had to do some serious wrestling with issues of faith, and I eventually came to the rather obvious conclusion that you cannot know if God is trustworthy until you test it out and live as if God is dependable. You can never learn to drive a car until you get in and actually drive it. So it is with faith.

Later in my studies I encountered an intriguing idea called *Deus absconditus*. This postulates that in some ways God hides from us. We should not expect the heavens to be ripped apart so that we can see God's face. We should not plan on God coming to the rescue every time we get ourselves into a problem. This is one of those cases where we end by saying: God just does not work that way. One of the keys that opened the door for me comes in Romans 1. Paul is beginning to make his case that all persons should know two facts, that God exists and that human beings sin. He writes, "For what can be known about God is plain to them, because has shown it to them. Ever since the creation of the world his eternal power and divine nature, invisible though they are, have been understood through the things he has made." (1: 19-20) He argues that simply looking at the world reveals two important qualities of God, his power and divinity, and that should be obvious to all. I know many people who can look at a sunrise and say that that event affirms their faith in God, but I also know people who find no call to faith in that same event.

Consider these two instances. The nineteenth century English poet Matthew Arnold describes standing at the sea shore one night watching the waves. The sight generates no faith in him. He writes, "But now I only hear/Its melancholy, long, withdrawing roar/retreating...down the vast edges drear/And the naked shingles of the world." The sight that Paul would claim should call forth faith in God for Arnold only produces melancholy about the apparent lack of purpose or divine presence in life.

Contrast that with the writer of Hebrews. "Now faith is the assurance of things hoped for, the conviction of things not seen." (11: 1) What follows is a roll call of Old Testament saints, people who lived by faith in God and found assurance and vindication in that faith. For this writer faith could be nurtured by looking at the hosts of people through the ages who have lived by faith and found God to be as steadfast as a rock.

We are back, then, to my thought that to have faith you must try it out. My wife and I have been married forty-three years. I can with full confidence say that I have faith in my wife. In fact, I would trust her with my life. When we first started going together we were testing out our faith in each other, and little by little we found each other to be trustworthy. It works that way with God.

One of heroes mentioned in that role call of faith in the book of Hebrews is Gideon. His inspiring, truthful, and sometimes funny story can be a model of faith for us. After the people of God had settled in the land of Canaan they did not form a government, but rather functioned as a loose confederation of tribes. From time to time other tribes in the area would gather together and attack the Israelites, and sometimes even conquer them. At these times of disaster God would call forth a leader to defend the people of Israel. They were called judges and their stories are found in the Old Testament book of that same name. These men and women sometimes settled disputes in the sense that we today use the word judge, but they were also military and political leaders always called and guided by God.

One of the most unlikely of the judges was Gideon. You can find his stories in Judges 6-8. The threat at this point comes from the Midianites, a neighboring country, which had attacked and prevailed over Israel. Many of the Israelites went into hiding, waiting for better time. We meet Gideon first as he is trying to thresh wheat in a wine press. Now remember that threshing works only in the open where the breeze carries off the chaff. Constrained by his fear of the enemy, Gideon is trying to do the impossible, trashing wheat in a hole in the ground. And angel appears and greets him with a stunning announcement, "The LORD is with you, you mighty warrior." (6: 12). Gideon replies sarcastically: if God is with us why are we in this mess. I would think sarcasm with an angel is unwise. The fact is that Gideon does not recognize who he is talking to. The angel nevertheless commissions Gideon to deliver Israel from the hand of Midian. Gideon responds by noting that he is the lowliest member of the weakest tribe of Israel.

Sensing his doubt, the angel tells Gideon to stay where he is until he, the angel, returns. Meanwhile, Gideon practices the customary hospitality and prepares a meal for the angel, who eventually returns, touches the meal with the end of his staff, and flames shoot forth and burn up the meal. Gideon finally gets the point. "Oh, I have encountered an angel and I probably will get burnt up, too." God speaks: no, Gideon, you will not die. So far, we have hardly seen any faith at all in this shy and lowly man.

God then instructs Gideon to sacrifice a bull, but the twist is that he is to cut down a pagan totem pole erected in honor of the Midianite fertility god Baal, and use the wood in his sacrifice. Gideon does as commanded, but does it under cover of darkness, because he is afraid of his family and the townspeople.

The situation turns more desperate. The Midianites are joined by the Amalekites, and both begin to march into Israel's territory. We are told that the spirit of God took hold of Gideon, who found enough courage to call for the men of several Israelite tribes to join him in fighting their enemies.

But Gideon soon goes back to his default position. He proposes to test God. He says, "God, to see if you really will deliver Israel, I want to do the following. I will tonight lay out a sheep fleece on the ground, and if you plan to deliver us, in the morning the fleece will be wet with dew but the ground will be dry." The next morning the ground was, indeed, dry, and Gideon wrung a bowl full of dew from the fleece. God had passed the test, but that was not enough for our man.

Gideon again says to God, "Don't be angry, but I need another test. This time the fleece should be dry but the ground covered with dew." And the next morning it was as Gideon asked. Only then did Gideon find the strength to lead the forces of Israel.

The story continues with other fascinating episodes, and in the end the enemies flee for their lives from the land of Israel. As I said earlier, I find this a laugh-out-loud story, but I find it also appealing and helpful.

First, Gideon did not easily acquire faith. He needed to test the ground of faith. Furthermore, he was not afraid to admit this and take his doubt to God. The issue for Gideon was not the existence of God. The issue, rather, was the dependability of God. Did God really favor Israel, and would God act to deliver Israel? Gideon wanted to know the character of God.

These remain relevant questions today. Many people talk about God, but the real issue is what God is like. Is God indifferent? Is God aware of what goes on with people? If God does care, can God act on that? Will the end result be blessing or curse?

Also, Gideon knows that his fate depends on the steadfastness of God. What if he ventures forth in faith, and finds that God is not dependable? If that were to happen he would likely die in battle. Faith is always a deadly serious matter. What can you trust?

God initiates the faith process. Gideon is minding his own business in the wine press when the angel announces from the start what Gideon will be: "The Lord is with you, you mighty warrior." One of the consistent patterns of scripture is that God takes the initiative in regards to forging a relationships. Many of the Bible's stories narrative dramatic event, for example, Paul's conversion on the road to Damascus. (Acts 9: 1-9) On the other hand, sometimes coming to faith is a far less dramatic affair. In the little epistle of 1 Timothy, the writer urges young Timothy not to neglect the gift of the Spirit given through prophecy (read preaching) and the laying on of hands. But in any case, it is God who steps forward and reaches out to us. For us this sense of God reaching out to us happens most vividly in the great and primary sacrament of baptism.

Finally, God proves himself worthy of trust. Gideon tested, and God fulfilled the promise of Gideon becoming a mighty warrior. Again, this constitutes the consistent pattern of the Bible. In the Old Testament perhaps the most common attribute of God is said to be divine steadfast love. And in Jesus this is brought to stunning fulfillment in the resurrection, the sign that nothing can separate us from that steadfast love of God.

Examine your life. Who do you trust?

Faith

DISCUSSION QUESTIONS

First, look through your calendar and calculate where and when you spend most of your time and energy? How does that comport with your faith in God?

Two, on what do you spend your money? Does that align with your trust in God?

Three, what is the connection between faith and commitment?

Four, besides Jesus which character in the Bible is for you a good example of faith? What person in your life today exemplifies faith in Jesus?

chapter 9

Forgiveness
The Healing of Relationships

Do you have childhood memories of something that seemed insignificant, which, nevertheless, sticks in your memory? I have one of those regarding forgiveness. I do not remember the circumstances except that I was small and that the man speaking was angry. He said, "I can forgive, but I can't forget." That comment confused me then, and still does today.

We know that forgiveness holds an important place as a theme of the scriptures and of the teaching of the church. But at the outset I must say that I do not believe it can be either easily understood or lived. You have to experience it and then reflect on it in order to appreciate and understand it. Thus, the stories from the Bible help us live into this important concept.

We begin, then, with a quick survey of the Bible. In the Hebrew of the Old Testament we find three terms translated as "forgiveness." These terms suggest the following:

- To cover or blanket,
- To lift up or take away,
- Or to send away.

Hebrew is a language of tangibles and uses many concrete and common-sense images. Given that, note that the three terms carry the idea that God can lift sin, or cover it up, and simply send it away. For example, the sacrificial system of the Jerusalem Temple operated on this level. The annual atonement ritual involved the high priest placing his hands on the head of a goat, thereby placing the sins of the people on the animal, which was then driven into the wilderness. In this way God lifted up the sin of the people, put it on the head of a goat, and drove it away. That was the way forgiveness happened.

The Greek of the New Testament again uses three terms to convey the idea of forgiveness:

- To loose or release,
- To be gracious to someone,
- Or to let someone off.

You can see a continuity with the Old Testament images.

Recently here in Montana some train cars jumped the tracks in Glacier Park. That created a huge mess on one of the railroad's main lines. We can use that as a metaphor for our need for forgiveness. As many prayers of confession note we tend to do what we should not do, or fail to do what we ought to do, and we end up in a bad place. Relationships with God, with others, even with the earth itself are broken and sometimes even ruined. Any of the senses of forgiveness we have mentioned above would come as a relief. Forgiveness, in a sense, gets us back on the track of living as disciples of Jesus.

We all stand in need of forgiveness. We have done damage to others, and the results can be painful and destructive. That need of forgiveness and the sense of guilt that accompanies it become one of the pressing needs of our lives. It sticks with us and demands attention and, if possible, resolution.

A particular episode from Jesus' ministry can open a door of understanding on this complex issue. It can be found in Mark 2: 1–12. Jesus has returned to his home base in the town of Capernaum, and hordes of people crowd around the house where he is staying. Four men appear carrying a paralyzed man on a pallet. Because of the press of the crowd they cannot get to Jesus, so they climb to the roof of the house, remove part of the roof, and lower the man in front of Jesus. What an extraordinary scene this is! Jesus looks at the paralyzed man and makes a remarkable statement to him: "'Son, your sins are forgiven.'" Some of the official teachers of the law, biblical scholars in effect, begin to question why Jesus thinks he is in a position to forgive anyone of anything. And, we must say, they have a point. We need to recall that in Jesus' culture infirmity was a sign of sin; either the man himself or perhaps a close relative had sinned and his paralysis was, therefore, punishment. Jesus asks the teachers which is easier, to forgive or to heal. Then we come to the climax: "'But so that you may know that the Son of Man has authority on earth to forgive sins'—he said to the paralytic—'I say to you, stand up, take your mat and go to your home.' And he stood up and immediately took the mat and went out before all of them." (2: 10–12) And all those gathered there are astonished and praise God.

The story helps us see that forgiveness is healing, healing of a relationship with God and with others. The paralytic is returned to the bodily state God desired for him. Notice that Jesus here does not tackle the issue of disease as a sign of sin but works with the common assumption that this is the case.

We also learn from this story that forgiveness is a wholistic matter. We know that we are a somatic unity, that body, mind, spirit, will, and imagination are intimately linked. Who of us, for example, has not had stomach cramps or a headache as a result of stress. The story supports that mind-body unity.

It also points to the condition of not being able to help ourselves. The paralyzed man had to have four friends carry him. This helpless state is often the arena in which forgiveness alone can operate. We all reach a place where we have to say "It is my fault and mine alone." We begin to sense the power of forgiveness when we reach this place.

Finally, the story allows us to see that only the offended can offer forgiveness. In the story, the major point is christological, that Jesus really can speak for God because he is the incarnation of the divine. When the paralytic is first presented Jesus addresses him as "Son." That stands as a hint of the forgiveness to come. God can restore and heal the broken relationship, symbolized in the man's broken body, by the pronouncement of forgiveness.

This story reminds us that forgiveness finds its roots in the very nature of God. A story in the book of Exodus portrays this for us. Beginning in chapter nineteen the children of Israel have been wandering in the desert after their release from slavery in Egypt. They arrive at the foot of Mt. Sinai and camp there. God declares his intention to establish a covenant, a solemn and formal relationship with these people whom God has rescued from slavery and from destruction at the Red Sea. God recalls the gracious act of release and rescue and promises to treat the Israelites as "my treasured possession out of all the peoples." (19: 5). In chapter twenty God delivers the Ten Commandments, which represent the people's side of covenant. While

God is giving the Commandments to Moses at the summit of Sinai, the people below have made the image of a calf out of gold and have declared it their god. (chapter 33) This, of course, violates the covenant, that is, it denies the special relationship which God has initiated. Moses in anger tosses down the stone tablets on which the Commandments have been written, thus destroying them, and God threatens to wipe out the Israelites. Moses intercedes and God relents. In chapter thirty-four a spectacular event occurs, especially in light of the sin of idolatry just committed by the people. God passes before Moses and pronounces God's special name. Remember in the ancient world of Moses to know someone's name meant you had knowledge of that person, were in relationship, and had some power of that person. In an act of gracious self-disclosure God reveals his name. In Hebrew it is YHWH, which in English Bibles is always translated as LORD. The name is based on the "to be" verb, and roughly means I am who I am, or I will be who I will be. But just as God again passes before Moses and discloses the divine name, God states who he will be. "The LORD passes before him, and proclaimed, 'The LORD, the LORD, a God merciful and gracious, slow to anger, and abounding in steadfast love and faithfulness, keeping steadfast love the thousandth generation, forgiving iniquity and transgression and sin.'" (Exod 34: 6–7) The very nature of God, that which most characterizes God, is forgiveness. And, furthermore, forgiveness itself represents an act of extending to human beings the steadfast love of God. With that we reach one of the great moments in all of scripture!

All that is incarnated in Jesus Christ. He exists as God reaching out to humanity by assuming full humanity. At Jesus' death we see a demonstration that God's steadfast love has no limitation, and in his resurrection we realize that God's love cannot be defeated by any power.

I hope that in looking at the scriptural vocabulary of forgiveness and stories of forgiveness you can begin to sense the central role that forgiveness plays in human existence.

In closing, I offer five facts of life about forgiveness. First, it calls for awareness of who we are. As baptized persons we have the life-giving promise that we belong to God always and forever. But we have to admit that we fall into sin, that we are simply in the wrong. This is not easy or simple admission for anyone. Yet it must be stated. The classical statement of this position is "simul justus et peccator." That means: I am simultaneously a saint and a sinner, I stand as a sinner whom God in Christ chooses to see as a beloved child.

Second, it calls for a clear statement of forgiveness. I once attended an ecumenical worship service during which we all confessed our sin. But there was no absolution, no formal and clear statement that God forgives sinners. Not only do we need to be aware of who we are, but we also must know who God is. We need that know again and again God forgives, because God is steadfast love. This proclaims the truth on which we can and should build our lives. This represents the truth that opens up life so that that we can live with confidence and hope.

Third, forgiveness calls for amendment of life. I myself do not know how we can admit that we get it wrong, that we do not love God with all our being and our neighbor as ourselves, and yet not acknowledge that we can change the way we live. I have had people tell me, "This is the way I am, and people need to get used to it." A little honest reflection about one's self in the presence of God would change that. All the baptized are asked to be in a journey with Christ and toward Christ, and that means that we need to work at holiness, at integrating ourselves more and more into the mind of Christ.

Four, forgiveness calls us to realize that it is never cheap. This brings us back to the comment at the beginning of the chapter, "I can forgive but I can't forget." The point is to forgive even while you remember. That calls for the hard work of swallowing pride, of admitting a part in injuring others, of being vulnerable. Forgiveness is always cross-shaped, always involves some sort of sacrifice, always costs. Consider this case. Suppose you are the priest of a church in a small town, and one day you get into a yelling match at the local grocery store and you attempt to punch the other person. Word of the event spreads through the town. People in the congregation are upset at the lapse in your behavior. They are disappointed in you and the fear for the reputation of their church. You go to the vestry, explain your side of the event, and ask for their forgiveness. Does the vestry forgive or not? What would be the personal cost to each vestry member? What do the priest and vestry say to the community? If forgiveness is to happen, it will cost everyone involved. And not everyone will be willing to pay.

Finally, forgiveness calls us to change the past. I know that we think the past is what it is, that it is cast in stone. But forgiveness says that the past is not necessarily definitive for us, that we can be freed from its long arm. I have known couples where one partner has been unfaithful, and yet the other partner says that all is forgiven. When I hear that, I first sense the sacrifice that has been made by the offended person; he or she has had to give up a sense of revenge or a sense of self-righteousness. But beyond that, the offer of forgiveness changes the way the past works in the couple's lives. It has changed things. And only forgiveness can do that.

One more story says it all. In one of his parables Jesus tells of a son who wishes to escape the orbit of his family, and he crassly asks for his share of the inheritance from his father. In an act of great patience the father complies, liquidates assets, and gives money to his son. The son for his part goes far away, and quickly squanders his funds in wine, women, and song. To support himself he does what no self-respecting Jewish member of Jesus' audience would do, he takes a job of tending hogs, an employment that would put him in a state of perpetual religious uncleanness. He reaches the end of his rope and decides to go home and beg for forgiveness from his father. "But while he was still far off, his father saw him and was filled with compassion; he ran and put his arms around him and kissed him." (Luke 15: 20) Where does such compassion and forgiveness come from? Why would the father even want to accept again such a son? Such forgiveness can come only from the God whose very name is steadfast love.

DISCUSSION QUESTIONS

First, what do you see as the biggest issue in offering forgiveness? Why?

Second, do you find it hard to accept forgiveness? Why?

Third, in what ways do all sins result in ruptured relationships?

Four, Jesus tells us that what is expected of us is to love God with our whole being and to love our neighbor as ourselves. How does this make you feel? How does forgiveness play into this?

chapter 10

Gifts of the Spirit
Open your Gifts!

YEARS AGO I OFFERED a short Saturday retreat on gifts of the Spirit. One of the participants was a long-time, active, and beloved member of the congregation. I tried to explain the concept of gifts to those present, and we moved on to consider what gifts we might have been given. This woman said, "Why, I don't have any gifts of the Spirit." The others responded quickly. "Oh yes you do!" they shouted. Then various people begin to list what they saw in this woman that seemed to be spiritual gifts. The list was long and rich.

On the other hand, we run across a very different situation in 1 Corinthians. Paul writes, "In every way you have been enriched in him, in speech, and knowledge of every kind…so that you are not lacking in any spiritual gift." (1: 5, 7) But that was exactly the source of their problem. They were engaged in words and deeds that divided that church, because everyone thought they themselves had more and better gifts than others. Paul nails the problem in chapter 13. The gift they lack is love, the greatest and most essential gift of all.

We vacillate between poles of feeling we have nothing to offer and of believing that we are better and more gifted than others. We need to step back and clarify what we mean by gifts of the Spirit.

In the Old Testament only prophets and kings were believed to receive spiritual gifts. This marked the person as having a special relationship with God with the result that they were empowered by speak on behalf of God or rule the people on behalf of God. Only in the prophecy of Joel do we find a different view. Joel foresees the day when all people will receive the Spirit, young and old, women and men, free and slave, so that all will have a special relationship with God and all will be prophets. (3: 28-29)

In the Greek of the New Testament the word translated as "gifts of the Spirit" is *charismata*. It means an outpouring or anointing with the invisible but real presence of God. In both Old and New Testaments this outpouring was associated with the act of anointing a person with olive oil, and the church today continues to anoint people at "Holy Spirit" occasions, at baptism, at times when healing is needed, and at ordinations

To speak of the Spirit means to speak of the presence of the Risen Christ, who lives beyond time and space and is available always to all people. These gifts consist of skills, talents, and interests that Christ can consecrate for his work in the church and the world. The gifts are manifest outwardly in actions and deeds. The action of the Risen Christ bestowing spiritual gifts on the baptized serves as the life blood of the church.

I have already pointed out issues about the Spirit of Christ in the ancient church in Corinth. A quick review of that situation and Paul's response will help us grasp more clearly the way that the Spirit works in lives.

First, some gifts are basic, necessary and given to all. In 1 Cor 12: 3 Paul declares that no one can make the basic Christian confession of Jesus is Lord without the Spirit enabling that. Faith itself is the result of the working of the Risen One in our lives.

Second, gifts come in a variety of forms but are all given by the one Spirit. Paul lists some of these: wisdom, knowledge, faith, healing, working miracles, prophecy, discernment, tongues, and the interpretation of tongues. (12: 10) But a crucial point is this: "To each is given the manifestation of the Spirit for the common good." (v. 7) Paul wants to acknowledge the many gifts at work in the church in Corinth, but he also wants to puncture any sense of pride and personal possession that these may bring. Hence, he notes the common source of the gifts, the Spirit, and the common goal, the good of the church.

Continuing his discussion of gifts, the apostle states that these gifts are given in and through the sacraments. "For in the one Spirit we were all baptized into one body---Jews and Greeks, slaves and free---and we were all made to drink of the one Spirit." (12: 13) Any discussion of sacraments must point out that they are means by which the Risen Christ makes himself present. And this, in turn, suggests just how important the sacraments are to the life of the church.

Next, some gifts are given to those who exercise various offices in the church. It is a gift that some are apostles, some prophets, some teachers, some workers of power deeds, some have the gift of healing, some offer assistance, and some have leadership gifts (in the Revised Standard Version this last is translated as the gift of administration). (12: 27-28) So both individuals and the church can be recipients of God's gifts, and all are for the purpose of carrying out God's ministry. We might well imagine Paul whispering under his breath: "They are for ministry, not for bragging about or to make you feel proud of yourself."

In chapter fourteen we find Paul's discussion about speaking in heavenly tongues, in Greek, *glossolalia*. This is not a matter of being good at learning and speaking a foreign language, although in my mind that is also a gift. Rather, heavenly tongues is speaking in a manner unlike any human speech. While I have not been given this gift, I certainly have prayed with people who do. The result is a series of sounds often using la-la utterances, clicks, and the like. It has a pleasant and even musical quality. I will venture a personal theory about this. I think the gift releases a person from the restraints of normal language, such things as vocabulary and grammar, so that the person in effect uses a sort of scat singing in praise of God. My experience of listening to people speaking in tongues points to an alternative way to praise God, unfettered by the usual customs of communication.

Paul notes that *glossolalia* was a common component of worship in Corinth, and he claims to have the gift himself. He, however, also notes that the only one edified by speaking in tongues is the speaker. It does not advance the common good, and, furthermore, leaves visitors completely outside the experience of worship. So, he insists that no one speak in tongues unless someone present can interpret the tongues for the congregation. Further, he demands that all this must take place in good order, not in jumble of people making their utterances together.

But the stunning climax of Paul's discussion arrives in chapter thirteen, one of the most beautiful, moving and profound passages in all the Bible. It is his description of God's sacrificial love demonstrated fully in the cross. After his discussion about the variety of gifts, he writes, "But strive for the higher gifts. And I will show you a more excellent way." (12: 31) Without love prophecy, knowledge, faith, even martyrdom are nothing. Then follows a detailed description. Love is patient, kind, not arrogant or rude, does not insist on its own way, it is not resentful, rejoices in truth, and endures all things. Love is eternal, even while the other gifts pass away over time. "And now faith, hope, and love abide, these three; and the greatest of these is love." (v. 13) Who would disagree? Love is the greatest of the spiritual gifts.

The other great source of insight about the Spirit can be found in the gospel of John. Beginning at chapter fourteen Jesus begins what we today refer to as the Last Discourse. It consists of final words to his disciples, followed by the great high priestly prayer in chapter 17. John's perspective is unique and worthy of a quick review.

Throughout this discourse Jesus calls the Spirit by the title of *paraclete*. It is translated in various ways, such as advocate, comforter, counselor; the basic sense is the one who stands up with you in court and pleads your case. In 15:17 he calls it the Spirit of truth. Remember that earlier in 14.6 Jesus refers to himself as the truth, suggesting that the Spirit is, in fact, the presence of the Risen Christ.

Then Jesus begins his portrait of the Spirit. It will teach you and will remind you of all that Jesus has said. (v. 26) The Spirit will prove the world wrong about sin, righteousness, and judgment. Sin in this gospel means not believing in Jesus; the Spirit will demonstrate that this is mistaken. It will show that Jesus was righteous in the sense Jesus and the Father are one, and, thus, Jesus is right in his teaching. And the Spirit will judge the ruler of this world as condemned. (16: 8-11) In summary, the Spirit will work to justify and uphold all that Jesus has said and done.

The Spirit will guide the church into all truth, and will glorify Jesus. (16: 13-14) Again, recall that Jesus has named himself as the way, the truth and the life in an earlier passage. (14:6)

John's gospel continues with Jesus' betrayal, trial, crucifixion, and burial. In chapter twenty we share in the story of the biggest surprise in human history. On the third day after his death, Jesus is raised from the dead. The disciples find his tomb empty, and then there follows a series of episodes in which the Risen Lord appears to his followers. They recognize him, they see him, and they touch him. On Easter evening the disciples are huddled in fear in a locked room, perhaps the room where days earlier they had shared in the Last Supper. Jesus appears, gives them the gift of peace, shows them his hands and side. And then he says, "As the Father has sent me, so I send you. When he said this, he breathed on them and said to them, 'Receive the Holy Spirit. If you forgive the sins of any, they are forgiven them; if you retain the sins of any, they are retained.'" (20: 21-23) Previously Jesus has taught about the Spirit in exalted terms, but now he actually gives the gift of the Spirit to the disciples. The act of breathing on them recalls the Old Testament passage in which God breathes life into the inert body of Adam (Genesis 2: 7). The new creation is thereby inaugurated.

As if that were not enough, Jesus then passes on his ministry to the incipient church gathered in that room. He sends them off with the Father's commission, and he passes on to them the authority to forgive and retain sins. I find this both stunning and awe inspiring. The church can become lackadaisical about it work and identity, but this passage is a dose of a powerful tonic. What we have here is that the church is the dependable dwelling place of the Spirit, and that comes about with the commission and authority of Jesus Christ himself.

By way of finishing this chapter, I offer some summary insights. First, you cannot detect the Spirit as a feeling. As you have seen there is nothing in scripture to suggest that the Spirit is accompanied by emotion, even though I hear it as a common sentiment. "Can't you just feel the presence of the Spirit?" No, you can't. You can spot the presence of the Spirit by what happens in the life of the church and of individual Christians. As we have learned, when someone has a sense of sin, that is the work of the Spirit. When someone speaks up for Jesus, that is the work of the Spirit. Watch the work; that will validate the presence of the Spirit, not feelings.

The work of the Spirit is best perceived in hindsight. Life goes by quickly as we experience it, but when we take the time to remember and to ponder we can point to the work and presence of the Spirit of the Risen Christ. I was once involved in a time-line exercise. We were given a long sheet of shelf paper and asked to draw a line down the middle of it. On the top of the line we were to mark important events in our lives, such as birth, first day in school, confirmation, etc. Below the line we were to mark the times when we were keenly aware of the presence of Jesus with us. The upper part of the line forced us to look back, and the lower part asked us to remember the past in a particular way. It did not take long to fill up the chart!

It energizes me to think that the church and I are part of the great, grand work of the Spirit. I find it easy to get bogged down and discouraged, but the scriptures ask us to look up and see the bigger picture. For example, sometimes I have the task of washing dishes. Most of the time I am looking down at dirty pans and junk floating in the water. But when I look up and out of the window, the view is something else altogether. I see the azure sky above the Rockies, the Big Belt mountains, the Missouri River, and an alpine valley. The thought of the presence, activity, and energy of the Spirit inspires me, and I hope you. Look up and see the Spirit at work.

DISCUSSION QUESTIONS

First, when were you first aware of the Spirit in your life?

Two, how do you sustain the presence of the Spirit in your life?

Three, in worship when are you most aware of the Spirit?

Four, how can you help your church "clean its windows" so that people can see the presence of the Spirit?

chapter 11

God
Above and Beyond

SOME YEARS BACK MY wife and I made a visit to the Grand Canyon. As far as the eye could see was an infinite variety of color and detail. It, in fact, simply beggars description. She and I were standing at one of the look-out points quietly enjoying both the view and the sense of awe evoked by the canyon. A woman and her teen-age son walked behind us, and as they did so, the boy said in a loud voice, "This is so boring." With anger his mother replied, "No, it's not!"

My wife and I were stunned that anyone would find the Grand Canyon boring. What had gone wrong with that young man? I suspect that he simply wanted to be with his friends doing something they considered interesting.

God is vast. God, too, beggars description. But for some people, God seems irrelevant and does not connect with their interests. I do not wish to be harsh, but I must say that to me this point of view, like that of boy at the Grand Canyon, is far too self-focused and small. The tiny and self-interested frame of reference simply filters out God.

Most people in most of human history, however, have assumed the existence of God. The question of whether God exists or not was simply a non-question. We can this is ancient attitude at work in the scriptures. In Psalm 44 we find these words: "Rouse yourself! Why do you sleep, O Lord? Awake, do not cast us off forever! Why do you hide your face?" (Ps 44.23-24) The non-existence of God is not posited as the reason for the psalmist experience; the problem is, rather, that God appears no longer to care about and hear the prayers of the psalmist.

Paul offers an even more compelling example. In the first section of his magisterial letter to the Romans, he argues that all persons are sinners and have not lived as God intends. He begins his case by saying that everyone knows about God. He writes, "For what can be known about God is plain to them, because God has shown it to them. Ever since the creation of the world his eternal power and divine nature, invisible though they are, have been understood and seen through the things that he has made." (Rom 1: 19-20) He can make this argument only because he assumes everyone believes in a divine being, who created all and whose nature is perceived in that creation. That was, after all, the assumption of most ancient people.

But ever since the advent of the Enlightenment the existence of God has been an issue. Part of this was based on a high evaluation of human reason. Descartes, for example, noted, "I think, therefore I am." But you see the problem, I hope. How can our minds grasp the one who is above and beyond all things, including our intelligence. If you can find a light-free zone and go there on a clear night, you can see the stars in full display. I have to admit I have been in such a place only once, and what I saw in the darkness left me awestruck. Understanding God would be like the ability to count all those stars.

Years ago I watched a TV interview with the later philosopher Mortimer Adler, who said that proving the existence of God was not hard, and he wrote a book entitled *How to Think about God* demonstrating that. Over the centuries various theologians and thinkers have developed proofs for the existence of God. We can consider a couple of them.

One is called the ontological proof. This, along with most of the others, depend on some form of syllogism. So, here is the argument: first, the universe had a beginning; second, all beginnings must have a cause; therefore, the cause of the universe is God. You may or may not find that convincing. But consider some ideas current in physics. Many scientists speak about the beginning of the universe as the Big Bang, a sudden expansion of energy that continues today. The puzzling factor is that energy left to itself runs out; that's called entropy. Might not one conclude that God caused the Big Band and still functions as a cause for the continuing existence of the cosmos?

And this leads to another proof, called the continuing case. Briefly it states that a dependent universe must have an independent being to continue, and that independent being is God.

The teleological proof is even more intellectually spectacular. First, if God exists, God must be conceived as a necessary being. Second, by definition, a necessary being cannot not exist. Therefore, if a necessary being can exist, then it must exist. Voila! God.

Others proofs develop in similar ways. There is a moral law at work in the cosmos, so there must be a great moral law giver. Another proof notes that the universe has a design, so there is necessarily a great designer.

I am not certain that "proof" is the right word. I think a person can walk away from these statements not convinced about God, perhaps because they seem like mere intellectually clever games. I myself find them suggestive and helpful and am grateful for them, but my understanding is not overwhelmed by them.

Perhaps that is because the issue of God's existence is not simply an intellectual matter. Perhaps it is more of an existential matter. This past summer I visited our diocesan summer camp for senior high students. One night the schedule called for a camp fire, so we all gathered at the edge of a lake to roast marshmallows and to talk. One young man stood up and stated that he had come to camp as an atheist, but that now he was a believer. This stunned me. I had always seen the existence or non-existence of God as an intellectual question, but here was a person testifying that he sensed the living presence of God in the life and activity of a church camp. For him, it was a matter of the heart, not the mind. And I think he was right.

If that is true, we are at a place where we can turn the Bible and the question of the existence of a personal God, a God who not simply exists but who also acts in human affairs.

Indeed, the Bible is a record of and reflection on centuries of a God active in the history of Israel, in Jesus Christ, and in the church. The Bible stands as an interpretation of human experience in light of divine activity in history.

But the scriptures ask us to take a further step. Not only do these ancients writing record God's activities, but they can also serve as an overlay for our current experience. The Bible assumes that the God who was capable of acting in the past in certain predictable and reliable ways can do the same today. I was once part of a retreat in which our leader asked us to tell each other about how God had been active in our lives. We spend an inspiring morning doing this. The story I most remember came from someone who had had a life full of pain and tragedy.

Deserted by her mother she had been raised in a series of foster homes, some of which could only be called abusive. After high school her life seemed to consist of a series of lurches in one direction or another. She told all of this to her aunt, who simply said that she, the retreatant, should read Psalm 35. When she did so, she discovered that her life journey was reflected there, as well as her heart-felt cries for rescue. "You have seen, O LORD, do not be silent! O Lord, do not be far from me." (Ps 35:22) The Bible had captured her life and then posited it before the God who acts. Because the Bible can do this, we call it holy; it mediates God to us.

We now stand in a place where we can consider the three big, biblical declarations about God. First, God creates. In the first book of the Bible, Genesis, we have an ancient story about creation. You can find this in Gen 1:1-2:4. Over a span of seven days, God speaks our world into existence. Order comes out of chaos, light out of dark, and at the climax of the story God creates man and women in God's own image.

This account of creation represents the understanding of God held by the ancient Israelites. And it contrasts with other creation stories in the ancient Middle East. Most of those narrate life arising out of the struggle and warfare of various deities, some good and some evil. But in scripture God alone creates and the purpose is to bless. The narrative ends with these wonderful words: "God saw everything that he had made, and indeed, it was very good." (Gen 1:31) In summary, we find at the start of the Bible a God who creates, a God of light and life, a God who blesses, and a God whose works are very good, indeed.

At this point I need to add that the creation account in Genesis 1 represents a theological statement about God and the world around us. It is not a scientific account of *how* the world began, but stands, rather, as a theological statement of *who* and *why* the creation exists as it does. The creation account in Gen 1 originates from a time long before the rise of science and does not concern itself with the questions posed by science. For instance, note that on the first day of creation God creates light (Gen 1: 3), but not until the fourth day does God create the sun. Clearly chapter one cannot represent a scientific explanation of how the cosmos came to be, but it does represent the insight that God has ordered and blessed the universe.

The second great event of the Bible, an event that offers rich insight into the nature of God, occurs in the second book of the Bible, Exodus.

Indeed, that second great event is the exodus of the Israelites from bondage in Egypt and their escape at the Red Sea. The twelve tribes of Israel found themselves in slavery in Egypt for centuries when God raised up a new leader, Moses. Through him God set in action a series of events that ended with the pharaoh gladly releasing his slaves lest he suffer any more plagues inflicted on Egypt by God through the agency of Moses. Off into the desert the former slaves flee, but in the meantime, pharaoh changes his mind and sends out his army to bring the Israelites back. The great crisis then happens. They arrive at the shore of the Red Sea with water in front of them and a hostile army pursuing from behind. Here happens the great event of the Old Testament. God sends winds which part the water of the sea, enabling the Israelites to flee to the other shore. When the army arrives they also charge into the parted sea, only to have the winds cease, and they are destroyed by the closing of the water over them. Jewish and Christian people have been mining the meaning of this story for millenia, and the results are rich, indeed. But we can come to at least these conclusions. The God of the Exodus acts to rescue and to liberate. Further, this God uses means; Moses and the winds, for instance, act as divine agents. That God does the same today.

The final great event of the Bible consists of the birth, baptism, death, and resurrection of Jesus Christ. In him God was acting in the most decisive way and continues to act whenever the story of Jesus is proclaimed. The first generation of Christians composed a hymn that summarizes the significance of Jesus.

> He is the image of the invisible God, the firstborn of all creation, for in him all things in heaven and on earth were created, things visible and invisible, whether thrones or dominions or rulers or powers—all things have been created through him and for him. He himself is before all things, and in him all things hold together. He is the head of the body, the church; he is the beginning, the first born from the dead, so that he might come to have first place in everything. For in him all the fullness of God was pleased to dwell, and through him God was pleased to reconcile to himself all things, whether on earth or in heaven, by making peace through the blood of the cross. (Col 1: 15-20)

Every phrase overflows with significance, but our purpose now is not to probe this passage but to highlight Jesus' life, death, and resurrection as the summit of God's workings among humanity and the paradigm for

God's continued activity today. If you are interested in a deeper exploration of Jesus read my book *Journey with Jesus: Encountering Christ in his Birth, Baptism, Death, and Resurrection*.

Later the church would summarize its understanding of God in the doctrine of the holy and undivided Trinity. Again, we are faced with exceedingly rich material that lies beyond the scope of this book. The most familiar access to the doctrine of the Trinity occurs in the Nicene Creed, a fourth century statement forged by two ecumenical councils of the church. It has stood the test of time and continues today as a source of intellectual and spiritual power.

The Trinity proclaims the existence of one, true God, who is apprehended and experienced in three ways. God creates and sustains the world; recall the earlier quote from Paul in Romans about the divine majesty and power seen in creation. God redeems and saves, granting the blessings of faith, hope, love, and life; Jesus lives as the door into this new reality. God is present and active as Spirit in the church, in the lives of God's people, in the forgiveness of sins, and in the hope of life everlasting. If nothing else, the Trinity says that God is complex, and that God's workings can fill life with meaning and hope.

We have reached a place where discursive writing cannot carry further the discussion about God. We enter the realm of art, music, and poetry, all of which open doors to the divine.

Think of a symphony by Bruckner or a fresco by Fra Angelico. Or ponder this ancient liturgical poem.

> Rank on rank the host of heaven, spreads its vanguard on the way,
> As the Light of Light descendeth from the realms of endless day,
> That the powers of hell may vanish as the darkness clears away.
>
> At his fee the six-winged seraph; cherubim with sleepless eye,
> Veil their faces to the Presence, as with ceaseless voice they cry,
> "Alleluia, alleluia! Alleluia, Lord Most High!"
> From the Liturgy of St. James, para. By Gerald Moultrie
> The Hymnal 1979, number 324

DISCUSSION QUESTIONS

First, have you ever had an encounter with God? If so, what did you think and feel?

Second, what biblical story especially helps you know and understand God?

Third, if questioned by a non-believer, how might you respond?

Fourth, make a list of the qualities of God that mean the most to you.

chapter 12

Grace
Better Than I Deserve

As a child we were sometimes invited to have dinner at my great aunt's home. She was from the mountains of West Virginia, and that fact showed in everything she did. I remember driving up to her house and she was in her front year picking dandelions. I found out later that those would be our salad for dinner that night. I was shocked that we were eating weeds, even though I found them tasty. She could tell the funniest stories, and she clearly enjoyed hosting us. Part of that culture was that a meal always included a stack of white bread, something that we did not do at home because my mother did not approve of that practice. So, we were having dinner and I was enjoying having bread with my meal; for me it felt like a special treat. I was reaching out for still another slice, when my mother intervened. My aunt spoke up, "Let the boy eat what he wants." I still remember those words as a sort of gift; this skinny little kid could have more bread. My aunt's name was Grace.

Grace carries many connotations, and can be understood in various, sometimes, contradictory ways. In ancient Rome it was used in the context of an extensive patronage system. It almost always suggested a favor from a superior to an inferior. For example, the emperor might grant a special dispensation, perhaps a special position to a political ally in order to curry favor. They called this grace.

But the Bible takes a very different slant on this key term. We have already looked at the creation story in Gen 1, and noted that God created a beautiful, fruitful world for the benefit of humanity; the story conveys that sense that God freely gives gifts.

Later we find likely the oldest poem in scripture; in it the prophet Miriam sings a song of victory after the Israelites have crossed the Red Sea. "Sing to the LORD, for he has triumphed gloriously; horse and rider he has thrown into the sea." (Exod 15. 21) She and the Israelites had prevailed against the Egyptians, but only because of God's action. God had granted the gift of victory.

Probably the most common characteristic of God as the people of Israel experienced God was steadfast love. It crops up in all the parts of the Old Testament. Those ancient people of God knew that divine favor was reliable, so that they could both establish their lives on it and could expect it in the future. The word "grace" sums this up in a single word.

In 1604 a new, very bright star appeared in the sky, and the great German astronomer Johannes Kepler gave it careful study and wrote about it. He called it a supernova. Today we know that such an event represents the end of a star, but for Kepler and his contemporaries it marked the beginning of a new light in the sky. Hence he gave it a Latin name: super new.

The New Testament records the great bursting forth of a new light, a new era of grace, with the incarnation of Jesus Christ. He appeared as the super new, and he marked the beginning of what St. Paul would later call the new creation. In Jesus, God's grace abounds. He becomes the epiphany, the shining forth, of divine steadfast love.

We can take a quick hope through the gospels to capture a sense of the grace Jesus mediated by Jesus. In Matthew's gospel we find the story of the visit of the Wise Men to the infant Jesus (Matt 2: 1-12) A star, which perhaps we might understand to be a supernova, guides the Wise Men to the one they see as the new king of the Jewish people. Certainly this episode wants to impress on us that God's grace is offered now even to foreigner, in this case astrologers from Iran. The light is shining forth on new horizons and new peoples.

Every Sunday school student learns about Zacchaeus, that notorious tax collector and sinner. His sin had many levels. First, he collaborated with the Roman conquers, who allowed him to collect as much tax as he could wheedle out of people. In doing so, he had to handle Roman coins, which put him in a perpetual state of religious uncleanness. Yet to him Jesus declares, 'I must stay at your house today." (Luke 19. 5) Later Jesus explains his action. "Today salvation has come to this house . . . For the Son of Man came to seek out and save the lost." (Luke 19. 9-10) God's favor can fall on even the most public of sinners.

In Mark's gospel we find another story about the surprise of grace. Jesus stands in the midst of a crowd when a woman touches him, and he senses that some of his power had passed on to this unfortunate woman. She had had a case of continual menstrual bleeding for a dozen years; this condition put her in a state of continual religious uncleanness, making her, therefore, outside the circle of God's concern. Further, Jewish women did not touch men in public, but even more shocking is that she talks with Jesus in the open. Thereby she had become a triple-threat pariah. But note Jesus's response, "Daughter, your faith has made you well; go in peace, and be healed of your disease." Light shines on the unlovely, and the circle of grace expands again.

Mark chapter four contains one version of Jesus calming the storm. He and his disciples are crossing the Sea of Galilee at night when a windstorm arose. The boat was being swamped, the disciples panicked, but Jesus was asleep in the stern. The disciples cry, "Teacher, do you not care that we are perishing?" (Mark 4. 38) Jesus instructs the storm to cease, and a dead calm ensues.

I myself was sleeping one night in the town of Tiberias in a hotel on the very shore of the Sea of Galilee, and the howling of wind woke me at about 3 AM. I went out on the balcony and saw huge waves, perhaps ten feet high, erupting on the surface of the lake. I have never seen anything to compare with wind and waves that night. I thought of this story, of the terror of the disciples, and especially of their question, "Do you not care that we are perishing". Does God care? Does God hear prayer? Does God act? This famous episode answers with the word of grace.

Finally, we must consider the appearance of the Risen Christ in John 20. It takes place on the evening of Easter day. We find a group of the disciples gathered in a room with doors locked out of fear. After all, Jesus had been executed by the authorities, and the rightly thought that they might well be next. Into this chamber of anxiety the Risen Lord is suddenly present, and a number of moments of grace follow. Jesus greets them with a word of peace, and then shows them his hands and side, thus proving that this is the Jesus they knew to have been executed. Then again comes the greeting of peace. Next, Jesus extends to his disciples his mission: "As the Father has sent me, so I send you". (John 20. 21) Jesus breathes on them, thereby giving them the Holy Spirit, and adds that they have the authority to forgive and retain sins.

I find myself coming back this this story again and again. Jesus moves his followers from fear and isolation to peace, power, and mission. Things always work that way when the Risen One is present. We call this the paschal mystery, the movement from death to life, fear to joy, isolation to mission. By virtue of baptism all Christians are joined to Jesus' death and resurrection, and thus share in the paschal mystery. What more gracious gift could God give?

I was about ten and was enjoying vacation Bible school at my church. My grandmother was the teacher of the class. One day the subject under discussion was grace, and she insisted that we memorize the classic definition. Here it is. Grace is the unmerited favor of God. Through the years I have come to see that day in Bible school as a moment of grace, because that definition has helped me interpret much of my life experience.

God chooses to bless us, not because we have earned it, and not because God is attempting to set up some sort quid-pro-quo arrangement. God simply chooses to bless, because God is by nature gracious.

Moreover, divine grace is always and everywhere dependable. That theme runs through almost any of the stories of scripture one might point to. God is trustworthy, and that, too, is part of God's nature. Faith stands as the factor that receives God's grace and trusts that God will continue to be gracious in the future.

Every Thursday night my great-grandmother would appear out our door. We had the nearest tv set, and she wanted to watch the Groucho Marx show. I remember her rocking in her chair and slapping her leg in laughter. The format was simple; two contestants would win money by correctly answering Groucho's questions. But the real point was conversations he had with those volunteers. The announcer would state the names of the two contestants, and then say, "Now come and meet Groucho Marx". They would come forward smiling, eager to be with him. As I watch reruns today I wonder why they were so eager. Groucho often skewered them with his wit or made them the butt of jokes. The show was entitled *You Bet Your Life*. And in a sense you did make that bet. You might well end your time with Groucho looking silly before the whole country.

Contrast that with God. Grace always endures as the key word to describe how God will act toward us, with compassion, blessings, and love. With God, you really can bet your life.

DISCUSSION QUESTIONS

First, can you state your own definition of grace?

Second, what moments of God's grace can you recall in your life and the life of your church?

Third, do you have a favorite grace story from the Bible?

Fourth, how could you and your church become agents of grace?

chapter 13

Holy Baptism
The Waters of Grace

WHEN I ENTER AN unfamiliar church I always look first for three things, the altar, the pulpit, and the baptismal font. In my mind these are the three items that make a room into a church. They each form the focus of the events that constitute worship: the reading of and preaching about the scriptures, and the actions of the Eucharist and Baptism. I usually have no trouble finding the altar, because it often is of such a size and location that it immediately draws our attention. And near the altar I can often spot the pulpit or ambo easily. The problem comes in finding the font, the place of baptism. It is often stuck away in a dark alcove in the back of the church or pushed into the shadows somewhere in the front of the church. I grant the more modern church buildings do not play "Hide the Font," but we have many that push the place of baptism out of sight and, therefore, out of mind.

Despite the message of our architecture, the sacrament of Holy Baptism represents a stunning act of God's grace. Indeed, it *is* the gospel in action and in deed.

The word in the original Greek of the New Testament simply mean to wash or to dip. The term was used for common activities such as cleaning the dishes. But early Christians adopted the word and transformed it into something both wonderful and profound.

In the gospels we encounter Baptism first in the ministry of John the Baptist. As a child I thought that his title indicated that he was a member of

Holy Baptism

the Baptist Church, but later recognized that it indicated a major characteristic of his work. John's preached fiery sermons calling for people to prepare themselves for a great act of God that was in the making. He anticipated God's approaching judgment, and he pointed to Jesus as God's unique agent of that judgment. Later the Baptists was surprised to learn that the coming judgement was one of love, not punishment.

John's urged people to make their repentance concrete in an outward act of baptism in the Jordon River. A common act of piety among Jewish people of that period was a ritual baths by which they cleansed themselves from impurity. For instance, touching a dead body made one ritually unclean, and thereby unacceptable to God. Ritual baths were easy to find and dipping oneself into one washed away impurity. So, the symbolism of baptism was quickly understood by the people. Furthermore, doing so in the Jordon recalled the ancient story of the Israelites entering for the first time into the promised land by crossing that river, thereby suggesting that they were entering a new spiritual landscape as part of God's chosen people.

But the washing associated with Jesus stands as an event in a different order. It exists as something more than an outward act symbolizing one's repentance. The paradigm for understanding this new washing is found in the stories of Jesus' encounter with John the Baptist.

All four gospels narrate the event, but we will together look at Matthew's account since it is the most detailed one. Here it is:

> Then Jesus came from Galilee to John at the Jordon, to be baptized by him. John would have prevented his, saying, "I need to be baptized by you, and do you come to me?" But Jesus answered him, "Let it be so now; for it is proper for us in this way to fulfill all righteousness." Then he consented. And when Jesus had been baptized, just as he came up from the water, suddenly the heavens were open to him and he saw the Spirit of God descending like a dove and alighting on him. And a voice from heaven said, "This is my Son, the Beloved, with whom I am well pleased. (Matt 3: 13–17)

Let's summarize what happens in this event. First, note that Jesus was baptized. This is so obvious that we may miss its significance. This is the initial act in hos public ministry, and that, in itself, should be a clue to its importance. Add to that the fact that God is involved in the baptism. We have moved beyond a symbolic act of an individual to an event in which God is the major actor.

Next, in his baptism Jesus receives confirmation of his identity. "You are my son" declares the divine voice. Clarity about one's identity stands as a basic issue that we all face again and again. Of all the things one could list as part of Jesus' identity, God makes clear the most basic and important factor.

His baptism affirms Jesus' standing before God. Jesus is the Beloved. Not only does he need to know who he is, but also that he is loved. In fact, Jesus' identity finds in foundation in the love of God.

Next, the descent of the Holy Spirit empowers Jesus. God promises by means of the baptism to be present with Jesus in his work. His connection to God is complete and whole, so that Jesus can serve as God's agent in powerful ways.

Finally, Jesus' baptism marks his as a man with a mission. The long tradition of the Old Testament was that the Spirit of God was given to prophets and kings, who were thus authorized and commissioned for their important ministry among the people of God. So, Jesus, now identified, affirmed, and empowered is prepared to carry out the mission of inaugurating God's kingdom as both the ultimate prophet and the ultimate monarch.

Here we need to pause and take a deep breathe. Consider that all that happened to Jesus in his baptism happens to us when we are baptized. We, too, are made into the daughters and sons of God. We, too, are promised that we are the beloved of God. We, too, are gifted with the presence of the Spirit. And we, too, are authorized to be agents of God's mission; we are the ministers and missioners of God's kingdom. All of this happens as an act of God in our lives. All baptized persons can point to a specific time and place when and where God ripped open the heavens and marked them as God's own forever. As I said, this is the gospel in action. It is no longer baptism with a small "b", a mere washing as a sign of our good intentions. It is now Baptism is a capital "B" as an indication that God has acted in a salvific was by means of water.

As if this is not enough, we need to add Paul's understanding. He overtly mentions Baptism seventeen times, and his characteristic phrase "in Christ" is shorthand for being made one with Christ through Baptism. Listen to his words from his letter to the Romans. "Do you not know that all of us who have been baptized into Christ Jesus were baptized into his death . . . For if we have been united with him in a death like his, we will certainly be united with him in a resurrection like his." (Rom 6: 3, 5) The imagery here is derived from baptismal immersion; down into the water as if you

Holy Baptism

are drowning, and then pulled out of the water into life. By Baptism, we are united to the death and resurrection of our Lord.

So the shape of Christian living is baptismal. The official name for this dynamic is called the paschal mystery. This means that God has promised that the pattern of our lives will be characterized by God being active in all the death-filled moments of our lives and moving us to a new place of life and hope. I am not suggesting this as an "everything will turn out ok in the end" nostrum. What I do mean is that God can take whatever happens to us and use it as a means of carrying out God's purposes for us, for the church, and for the world. The arc of the lives of the baptized always tends toward Easter. God continually is removing the stone that seals us in our dark and cold tombs. Honestly, have you ever heard a better promise?

Recently my one and only grandchild was born, and this gave his parents, my wife, and me great joy. They named this handsome and healthy boy Rowan. My daughter and her spouse have asked me to come to Los Angeles and baptize him later this year. Such factors as setting the date with their home church and getting permission of the local bishop need to be resolved. But when the time comes I will pack my bags, including a little bottle of Jordon River water, and head south. We will have a wonderful celebration. But most important is launching Rowan into a life of adventure with God, allowing him to be part of the paschal mystery, and revealing to him the amazing grace of God.

I had a friend, now deceased, whose favorite slogan was, "We'll just have to live into that." And that represents a challenge to those of us who are baptized. We need to visualize life as a matter of floating on the water of Baptism.

I sometimes present a task to church people. On paper put down a list of adjectives that identify you. Do it quickly. In my case, some of those descriptors are: husband, father, brother, male, American, college graduate. Given what we have said, is it not appropriate that the word baptized be at the top of the list? Does it not take precedence over all else?

I have an icon of Jesus' baptism on the wall of my office. When the afternoon sun light strikes it, the gold in the icon seems to shimmer with life. Part of the symbolism of icons is that the gold represents heaven. One of the striking aspects of the image in my office is that the water of the Jordon appears to have its source in the gold of heaven. Is that not true of our baptism as well? We are washed in the priceless water of God's heavenly grace.

DISCUSSION QUESTIONS

First, define baptism in your own words.

Second, think of ways in which you can more fully live into your baptism.

Three, baptism initiates an intimate union with Jesus, the crucified and risen one. How does this your view of yourself and of your fellow Christians?

Four, if you were going to design a church, where would you put the baptismal font and what would it look like?

chapter 14

Holy Eucharist
The Gifts of God for the People of God

WHEN I WAS A child I had a wish for every Sunday. I hoped that after church we would have lunch at my grandparent's home. I recall even sixty years later what was served and how delicious it tasted. But I also remember that as the eldest grandchild I had a seat at the "big table" and was able to hear all the stories and jokes that were part of the family lore. Often the meal ended with hot-from-the-oven pineapple upside-down cake topped with freshly made whipped cream, and I was even allowed seconds. To this day I cannot eat that without thinking of my grandmother.

Those Sunday events helped shape who I am. I was able to say to myself "This is my family and I know I have a place in it." I learned the family stories and was able to absorb the attitudes toward life that characterized my family. Little wonder I so eagerly looked forward to those meals.

The church has a family meal. It goes by many names: Holy Communion, the Lord's Supper, the Mass, the Mystical Supper. But perhaps the most commonly used title is Holy Eucharist. That is a Greek word for thanksgiving and it is related to the word for showing favor and rejoicing. At this meal the family gathers, we hear the family stories from the Bible, we pray, and eat, we rejoice, and we leave nourished and reminded that we have a place at the big table in God's family.

You might be surprised that the Eucharist has roots the run deep in the Old Testament. For example, to give thanks for the ancient people of Israel meant to situate one's self in the world, knowing that God is the maker of all things and, therefore, the owner of everything. So thanksgiving always stood as one of the basic parts of worship; it meant acknowledging that God is God and we are not.

The Old Testament uses a technical term that summarizes thanksgiving. The word is blessings. To bless God meant to name God as creator of all and to thank this unseen yet personal God for benefits freely bestowed on the earth and its inhabitants. Thus, "blessed are you, O God, maker of heaven and earth" was a typical way to begin prayers of thanks. You sense that that simple phrase carries weighty significance.

This serves, then, as a backdrop against which the church understands the Eucharist, the meal of thanksgiving and blessing. The church blesses God as the creator who provides for the needs of God's people. The Eucharist overflows with thanksgiving to the God who freely provides for and nourishes us.

The Eucharist finds its roots in the meal Jesus shared with his disciples on the night before he was betrayed. By this time, he knew that his death was imminent, and he deeply desired to share this last meal with his inner circle of followers. And it happened during the Passover festival with its memory of the Israelites being freed from slavery, the sacrifice of Passover lambs, families meeting to remember who they were, and, above all, that God acts to save and liberate. So the closest followers gathered with Jesus to bless, to thank, to remember, and recall who they were before God.

This eucharistic meal stands at the last step before Jesus sets off on his journey to the cross. As we ponder the meaning of his death, the Eucharist serves to interpret his passion, and vice-versa. The bread of the Eucharist symbolizes the broken body of our Lord and the wine his blood poured out. In the scriptures life was believed to reside in blood. Thus, Jesus' shedding of blood is the means of establishing God's new covenant. This covenant, this solemn relationship of love and forgiveness, is sealed in blood, in life itself, because it is a matter of life and death. This blood is made present in the Eucharist, and in our receiving it we are participating in the covenant wrought on the cross. The giving of Jesus' life is not an abstract event, something from long ago and far away, but is made present in the holy meal, and we, moreover, are offered it so that we might be participants in the covenant.

The Eucharist exists as a meal of remembrance. This is a second major factor in understanding this holy meal. In scripture, remembering is not merely recalling a fact, as, for instance, in my remembering where I left my car keys. Remembering, rather, means living into the past in such a way that it becomes a living reality. In a small way my grandmother's pineapple upside-down cake makes her present again to me, although she passed away over twenty years ago. The bread and wine Jesus offered his disciples two millenia ago in Jerusalem can become a present reality in the here and now. A prayer I use before the Eucharist says this: Be present, be present, O Jesus, our great high priest, as you were present with your disciples, and be known to us in the breaking of the bread. That's remembrance.

The death of Christ would have been just another tragic passing of a good man without the victory of the resurrection. And the Eucharist would be a vain act without the reality of the resurrection, without the fact that God raised the crucified Jesus from death into a new reality of life. Because of the resurrection, we can state that the Risen Christ is present in the bread and wine giving us his own resurrection presence. It is in this sense that we can speak of the bread and wine as the Body and Blood of Christ.

I hope you see that the Eucharist stands at the heart of the life and vitality of the church. To participate in it allows us the holy privilege of living into the gospel itself. The gospel proclaims that God is at hand, always ready to bless us with divine life and love, and this is exactly what transpires in eucharistic participation.

David H. C. Read was a famous Scots Presbyterian preacher of the previous generation. He served in the British army in World War II, was captured by the Nazis, and exiled into a concentration camp. He and the other captives were fed so little that they were slowly starving. He said that in those days he did not think about steak or lobster, rather he longed for simple bread. In a similar way, our world starves us, but in the Eucharist the one who called himself the Bread of Life comes to us and gives us the acceptance, hope, forgiveness, and love for which we desperately long.

We cannot overestimate the importance and significance of the Eucharist. In it we have an encounter of the divine kind. Such an event requires preparation and care, because in it we are meeting the one who loves us without limit and the one whom we love so much that we have committed ourselves to follow him. I remember my preparations for the senior prom in high school. There were flowers to order and pick up, a tuxedo to fitted, a car to clean up, a haircut to get. Those things were ways to prepare for a special event. In a similar way we need to prepare for the extraordinary event of the Eucharist. I suggest four factors.

First, remember that you are participating in Jesus Christ himself. He is present and we will bodily receive him. In a real sense, he will live in us and we will live in him. The following little poem can be found in many places, and it is often attributed to Queen Elizabeth I.

> Twas God the Word that spake it,
> He took the Bread and brake it;
> And what that Word did make it,
> That I believe and take it.

The Bread of Life by his presence makes our eucharistic bread the means of new life in him.

Second, emotions may or may not come into play. In my home church we had a member who would audibly weep when coming forward to commune and would throw herself with tears on to the altar rail. I was fascinated by that, because I did not understand it, and I still don't. During communion I sometimes have deeply emotional responses and at other times new insights into my relationship with Christ may happen. And there are times when I feel nothing, but simply depend on the promise that Christ is feeding me. In a similar way, I can experience delight in a trip to a good steakhouse but feel nothing eating a steak sandwich at my desk. In both cases I am nourished without reference to my feelings or thoughts.

To commune on the Body and Blood is to participate in the work and mission of Christ.

In Mark 10, Jesus has just told his disciples that he is on his way to Jerusalem where he will be rejected, suffer, and die. After that solemn announcement, James and John, two of his most devoted followers, approach Jesus to ask for a favor. They ask that when Jesus comes into his glory that they be granted the right to sit at his right and left hands. Jesus seems to be stunned. "You do not know what you are asking. Are you able to drink the cup I drink, or be baptized with the baptism I am baptized with?" (Mark 10: 38) To live in Christ implies that we will participate in his work and service.

Four, we bring all that we have and all that we are with us when we participate in the Eucharist. In The Episcopal Church the *Book of Common Prayer* instructs that the bread and wine to be used in the Eucharist are to be presented by representatives of the people at the time of the offering, and that the congregation is to stand as the gifts are presented. These acts help symbolize that what we are offering at the altar to be transformed by the presence of Christ represents ourselves. With the bread and wine we offer our joys, pains, concerns, hopes, and fears to Jesus, and in return he gives us himself hidden in the bread and wine.

For over forty years I have had the privilege of celebrating the Holy Eucharist. In the parish setting I could look out over the congregation, most of whom I knew very well. I could see the couple whose marriage was on the rocks, the man who had just been given a big promotion, the woman who had just learned she had cancer, the man caught in alcoholism, and the couple who had just become engaged. They were all there standing in God's presence. I have always put my best efforts into my preaching, and have tried, despite being an introvert, to be warm and accessible. But I also know that my sermons sometimes miss the mark, and that I am not able to be the sort of person some need. But I also knew that I would be able to place consecrated bread into the hands of each and say "The Body of Christ, the Bread of heaven." And that would be enough.

DISCUSSION QUESTIONS

First, can you recall a time when receiving communion was especially important for you?

Second, how might you better prepare yourself to participate in the Holy Meal?

Three, what would you say to someone who is indifferent to participating in the Eucharist?

Four, does eucharistic participation speak a word to racism, violence, and discrimination?

chapter 15

Holy Spirit

The Breath of God

I CAN STILL REMEMBER it. I could not have been very old, and I was playing with friends after a picnic in the city park. Being an awkward kid I managed to fall off the top of the slide and hit the ground with a thud. Panic set it. I could not move and I could not breathe. Maybe I was dying, I thought. Someone said, "You've just knocked the breath out of yourself." That explained things, but did little to ease the panic. No breath, no life.

In the Hebrew language of the Old Testament spirit and breath are the same word. So in the first creation story in Genesis 1 we find that "the wind of God swept over the face of the water." (Gen 1: 2) The footnote in the New Revised Standard translation says that the phrase can also be translated as "spirit of God."

In the next chapter of Genesis God molds a human form from the dust of the ground, then bends down and God 'breathed into his nostrils the breath of life, and the man became a living being." (Gen 2: 7) The breath and spirit of God both orders the world and also brings life. The breath and spirit of God is an extension of the active and powerful presence of God.

Here we note that if the spirit is from God and stands as an extension of God then we can properly say call it the Holy Spirit. As such, it brings about divine creative power and life.

As the story of the Old Testament unfolds the work and presence of the Spirit becomes more nuanced. In Numbers 11 we pick up a persistent theme in the story of the Exodus: the murmuring and complaining of the

Israelites during their desert journey. In exasperation Moses prays to God for some relief. Did I create these people, am I their nurse maid, he asks God. The response of God consists of Moses choosing seventy elders from among the tribes and then he took them to the Tent of Meeting. "Then God came down in a cloud and spoke to [Moses], and took some of the spirit that was on him and put it on the seventy elders, and when the spirit rested on them they prophesied." (Num 11: 25) The spirit/Spirit grants the gifts of prophecy and leadership.

After the Israelites settle in the promised land they are intermittently lead by persons called judges, although they were more likely to be military rather than judicial persons. At one point the king of Aram, that is, Syria in today's geography, forces the Israelites to serve the king. They cry out to God, who raises up Othniel to serve as a judge. "The spirit of the LORD came upon him, and he judged Israel; he went out to war, and the Lord gave King Cushan-rishataim of Aram into his hand." (Judg 3:10) The spirit/Spirt gives protection and victory to God's people.

Later God raises up a king as a permanent leader over Israel rather than the occasional judge. The first of those kings was Saul. As he becomes king he receives instructions from the prophet Samuel. Saul is to go to a certain town and there he will be met by a cadre of prophets. "Then the spirit of the LORD will posses you, and you will be . . . turned into a different person. Now when these signs meet you, do whatever seems fit to do, for God is with you." (1 Sam 10: 6–7) The spirit/Spirit brings the gift of leadership.

If we were plot out dozens of other instances we would find that the Holy Spirit brings leadership abilities, wisdom, protection, and victory, but these gifts are limited mostly to political and religious leaders, the kings and the prophets. In the Hebrew Bible the Spirit is bestowed on the few, not the many ordinary people.

But one prophet captures a vision of a new day with new blessings. Joel sees a day when God will test Israel with a plague of locusts. But beyond that he also envisions a time when God will do a new thing. "Then afterward I will pour out my spirit on all flesh, your sons and your daughters shall prophesy, your old men shall dream dreams, and your young men shall see visions. Even on male and female slaves, in those days, I will pour out my spirit." (Joel 2: 28–29) The life-giving, powerful, transforming, nearer presence of God, the Holy Spirit, will be given to "all flesh."

And with that vision we are ready to look at the Holy Spirit in the New Testament. In the chapter on Holy Baptism I deal with the Spirit of God poured out on Jesus at the time of his baptism. After all, the New Testament views Jesus as the preeminent prophet, priest, and king, who is also the whole people of God in one person and the new temple of God. The granting of the Spirit to Jesus by God confirms all those identities. But the Spirit is limited to Jesus alone. The day foreseen by Joel has not arrived yet.

Then the Lord is crucified, buried, and that would seem to end of the story. But God raises Jesus on Easter, and the story continues. In Luke's gospel the Risen Christ tells his apostles to stay in Jerusalem and they will soon be "clothed with power from on high." (Luke 24: 49) They do, and some forty days later the vision of Joel is fulfilled.

In chapter two of the Acts of the Apostles the coming of the Holy Spirit is narrated. The disciples along with Jesus' mother are gathered in one place when the Spirit descends with the sound of rushing wind and with the appearance of tongues of fire resting on each. They begin to speak in other languages, so that people from all the world can understand in their own speech. Next, Peter preaches a sermon in which he quotes Joel's prophecy, and then he proceeds to witness to Jesus' miracles, crucifixion, and resurrection. He urges them to repent and be baptized so that they might receive the forgiveness of sins and the Holy Spirit. As a result about three thousand people were baptized that day.

A more dramatic event would be hard to imagine. The Joel prophecy is fulfilled, people from all the world can hear the sermon, and Peter, the disciple who had denied Jesus three times, becomes a bold witness to what he has seen and heard. Baptisms occur, awe seizes the city of Jerusalem, and the disciples empowered by the Spirit now become the church.

Jesus himself knew this day coming. Under cover of darkness one of the leaders of the Jewish people, Nicodemus by name, had come to question Jesus. Jesus speaks of the time when people, all people, can become part of the new reality Jesus is ushering in. Jesus says to Nicodemus, "Very truly, I tell you, no one can enter the kingdom of God without being born of water and Spirit. What is born of the flesh is flesh, and what is born of the Spirit is spirit . . . The wind blows where it chooses, and you hear the sound of it, but you do not know where it comes from or where it goes. So it is with everyone born of the Spirit." (John 3: 5–6, 8) Note that the Spirit and baptism are connected, and by these means the Kingdom is open to all.

As Jesus approaches the time of his betrayal and death he teaches his disciples one last time. In part, he again looks to the new day of the Spirit and promises that he will send to them the Advocate, the Holy Spirit. And he summarizes what the Advocate will do. The Spirit will convict people of sin and show the world that the powers of sin stand condemned. It will show that Jesus is the righteous one who comes from and returns to the Father. Moreover, the Spirit will guide the church into all truth, and will always glorify Jesus. As a side note, let me point out that the Spirit is identified by what happens and not by feelings; we move beyond the witness of scripture when we try to point to the Spirit on the basis of feeling. We are able to identify the presence of the Spirit by hindsight, by looking for the signs of the Spirit's activity.

We can mark down some summary points. First, the Holy Spirit is given first to the apostles and then to all. The Spirit represents the power of God to make Christians, to birth the church. The workings of the Spirit are not private but happen as part of the life of the community of the baptized. Finally, the Spirit is quickly associated both with baptism and then with the laying on of hands, as, for example, in the ordination of the first seven deacons in Acts 6.

I collect fountain pens as a hobby. I recently bought a can of compressed air to clean dirt out of a pen. The can had bold print warning me to handle it carefully. The Holy Spirit is the compressed presence of the Risen Christ, and when present it does alter life. And we need to handle it with care, or, more accurately, allow the Spirit to do its careful work. We can't control it, and it will certainly challenge us and change us. My can of compressed air did its work, and my pen was as good as new. That's the way of the Spirit!

DISCUSSION QUESTIONS

First, define the Holy Spirit in your own words.

Second, can you identify times in your life when the Spirit has been especially active?

Third, given what you have learned how can you be more open to the working of the Holy Spirit?

Four, think of as many examples as possible of ways in which your church nourishes the life of the Spirit.

chapter 16

Holy Trinity
God Is Not Simple

GOD CAN BE DESCRIBED as a triple hypostasis related in a single ousia. In other words, God is a unity of differentiated particularities. Have you got that?

Those two sentences stand as an example of the difficulty of trying to grasp the critically important doctrine of the Holy Trinity. It lays out a uniquely Christian view of God, a view that sums up the biblical revelation about God. In prayer, in liturgy, in theology, wherever Christian people attempt to speak about God, trinitarian language comes to the fore.

We should not be surprised that the church's talk about God as trinity began with attempts to describe Jesus. If Christians were to speak of Jesus as both divine and human, how was he, then, related to God? Did Jesus only seem to be God, or was he God in the flesh? Was he one person with two wills, a divine will and a human will, or was his will perfectly united? Did God at some point in the life of the divine create Jesus, or was Jesus eternally a part of God? These sorts of questions occurred whenever early Christians proclaimed and taught the gospel in their culture. They sensed, rightly I believe, that the validity and truth of the gospel depended on careful replies to these issues.

Into the sometimes hot discussions of these questions stepped Constantine the Great (272–337), the Roman emperor. Although not baptized until he was on his death bed, he thought of himself as Christian, and for political reasons wanted to end the increasingly hostile ferment about Jesus

Holy Trinity

in his empire. In 325 AD he gathered the bishops of the church in Nicaea, a seaport town in Turkey. He understood this as an ecumenical, or universal, council of the church, and he viewed it as important enough for he himself to preside.

You can read accounts of the council of Nicaea, but you would need a chart to keep track of both the cast of participants and of the philosophical and theological positions that came into play. Some of the finest minds in the world were involved, people who were fully conversant with the intellectual positions of the time. And they naturally wanted to state the church's position in the philosophical language current at the moment. Our problem is that their language in not ours. Most of us, for instance, are not conversant with the nuances of Plato; these bishops and theologians were. Their work resulted in the Nicene Creed, the great summary of the church's belief regarding God. Just because their work does not immediately jump from the page does not mean we should not grapple with it. The plays of Shakespeare do not speak the language of today, but they are worth every effort to understand them.

We can, however, summarize their arguments in simple terms. God is one, but God exists as three persons known as Father, Son, and Holy Spirit.

The doctrine of the Holy Trinity is implicit in scripture. The Old Testament insistently declares that God is one, and Christians inherited that basic concept. But early Christians needed to account for their experience of both Jesus and the Holy Spirit. Note the passage from Paul's letter to the Romans. He is explaining life in the Spirit. "But you are not in the flesh; you are in the Spirit, since the Spirit of God dwells in you. Anyone who does not have the Spirit of Christ does not belong to him." (Rom 8.9) Note the manner in which Paul moves from God to Christ to the Spirit. He does not try to give careful definition, but you sense, I hope, thinking about God as three persons is already emerging in a document from the middle of the first century.

At this point I wish I had a moving story to tell about the Trinity. I do not. We are speaking of the interior life of God, so I would not expect anyone to have a narrative that pulls all the loose ends together. I wish I had a clever image or analogy that would make it all perfectly clear, but I do not.

But someone has said that the Trinity is as much a matter of prayer as it is theology. I believe that in our prayers we begin best to understand the Trinity. As we lay our lives before God in prayer, we begin to catch hints about the nature of God. As we pray and praise God, we sense that God is the generator and sustainer of all things. Until several centuries ago only one word could be used to describe God in this way: Father. I need to add that some passages in the Bible speak of God in feminine terms, usually as the one who cares and protects people. But pre-modern biology postulated that men generate life; hence, the scriptural and creedal statements about God. Today we can acknowledge both the truth of masculine and feminine images of God even while understanding that God is beyond both categories. But since scripture speaks of God as Father, that terms needs to be maintained.

What we know about God in a personal sense comes through Jesus Christ. The God of the Trinity is the divinity revealed by Jesus. So it was natural for Christians to pray to the Father "through Jesus Christ." Through Jesus we glimpse at God.

And in prayer we sense that the God revealed by Jesus has been active in the church and in individuals lives, but that presence is unseen. Only the word spirit can be used to name such an experience. So the church says that we pray to God through Jesus Christ in the power of the Holy Spirit. Prayer, then, has opened the door to an experience of one God in three persons.

In spatial terms we can say God is over us, in us, with and among us, but always for us.

We have arrived at a place where we can list five summary statements about God. First, God is not simple. If we get confused about the language of the Trinity, that might be the point. If God could be easily explained, then God would not be God. If you look at the Nicene Creed, for instance, you find that God is not defined as a being. That is too small, too narrow. God has to be beyond being, and even that might be too simplistic. The twentieth century theologian Paul Tillich used a poetic phrase to suggest this truth; he spoke of God as the ground of being. Do you find that helpful, or perhaps, not expansive enough?

God is not revealed or experienced in a single way. I live in the midst of the Rocky Mountains, and a look out my kitchen window on a sunny day would reveal the stunning Big Belt mountain range. Only God could create and sustain such majesty. And yet, I open my Bible and read about Jesus, and I find the nature of God also made manifest there. And I pray and sense that God is Spirit, unseen yet real and present.

Three, the teaching of the Trinity can be inferred from scripture. We find it in incipient form there. In the great mystical gospel of John again and again Jesus states that he and the Father are one; to know Jesus is to know the Father. And as Jesus prepares to die he promises that he will dispatch the Spirit to guide the church. (John 5: 19–20, 16: 7–15) While not explicitly stated as a doctrine in the New Testament, we see the first several generations of Christians beginning to develop that teaching.

Four, the revelation of Christ initiates the process named in the previous paragraph. In the gospel of Matthew, for example, the evangelist reaches back into the Old Testament prophecy of Isaiah in an attempt to describe Jesus; Matthew used the title Emmanuel (God is with us) to say something important about Jesus' identity. In an attempt to grasp who Jesus was the New Testament writes feel their way, so to speak, toward a trinitarian view.

Five, as I have said, the doctrine of Trinity grows out of prayer. When we contemplate the intersection of our story and the presence of God a trinitarian understanding becomes almost inevitable.

Over the centuries teachers have used analogies to help us grasp God as Trinity. Maybe the most familiar is St. Patrick and the shamrock. The legend says that he used that plant, consisting of one root and stem with three leaves, as a hint about the nature of God.

Others have spoken about the three states of matter. Water, for instance, can be steam, liquid, or ice, and yet remains water in all cases. So, too, with God.

Years ago I was in the Metropolitan Museum in New York. I had stumbled on to one of Rembrandt's famous self-portraits. The one there is especially moving: Rembrandt as an old man, painted in almost impressionistic style and with deep honesty. A trinitarian analogy took hold of my mind. Rembrandt created the portrait of himself, a full and intense one. So, we have the artist and his exact image. I can stand in that room in New York to study the image; indeed, it evokes something like prayer. That interaction between the portrait and my mind is a spiritual connection; something lively and genuine happens. So, we have, the artist, the portrait, and our interaction with the painting. Three parts in one. I have myself thinking about that afternoon again and again, and it has helped persuade me of the truth of the doctrine of the Holy Trinity.

My two daughters loved to ride around on a tricycle when they were young. I suggest that as we shape our lives as disciples of Jesus Christ, that we ride on a trinitarian tricycle. We can learn to live into the richness of God. The awesome land, sky, and sea call us to worship God. "Ever since the creation of the world [God's] eternal power and divine nature, invisible though they are, have been understood and seen through the things he has made," says Paul. (Rom 1: 20)

Contemplation of Jesus' words and deeds and especially his death and resurrection open to us the very heart of God. But we have been given the Holy Spirit, who works in and through our lives to pull us closer to God and each other. All of these experiences and many more ask to bask in the richness of our God. Knowing God is an endless journey of grace.

Our sense of God as Trinity provokes us to praise and worship. Sunday morning at church need not be a matter of fulfilling religious obligation, but can be living into the very life of God. Thanksgiving and praise mark the beginning of a genuine relationship with the Almighty.

And finally this. What Jesus reveals of the divine is that God is love. By that I mean the faithful commitment and care of God to us and for us no matter what we say or do. The scriptures call it steadfast love, a love you can build your life on, and love that vanquishes fear. If that is true, and I fervently believe it is, then we have to speak of the Trinity as the divine community perfectly united in love. Father, Son, and Spirit, eternally giving and receiving love, a love so grand that it pours forth into the whole creation. For us to live with even a touch of this self-giving love and commitment is to participate in the life of the Trinity. Let it be so.

DISCUSSION QUESTIONS

First, when did you first hear about God as Trinity and how did you react?

Two, can you find common analogies for the Trinity?

Three, the Trinity always points to the God who in the richness of love continually acts to bless us. Can you find evidence of that in your life?

Four, why might it be important to teach young people about the Trinity?

chapter 17

Hope
God's Future

IF YOU GOOGLE THE word "hope" one of the references that will appear is the phrase hope chest. It was a common item in a previous generation, and it usually consisted of a large, rectangular box that sat on the floor. Made of cedar it was carefully crafted. Young women were given a hope chest as a place to store their fine clothing in anticipation of marriage. It was a way to prepare for good future. It encapsulated hope.

For Christians hope connotes an attitude of heart, mind, and will in regard to the future. Hope postulates that God is preparing a good future for God's people. It stands as one of the most important and characteristic parts of Christian living, and, indeed, is considered one of the three cardinal virtues along with faith and love.

I live in Montana, a place of majestic beauty, a place that inspires awe and wonder. But we have a dark side. Montana has one of the highest rates of suicide in the country, and teen suicide stands at the top of the charts. Suicide can be caused by a tangle of factors, but usually despair and depression are at the top of the list. Life has become so intolerable that death seems the only way out. To put it another way, suicide means that all hope has drained out of person's life. Therefore, being possessed of hope represents an absolutely vital factor in our lives.

It should come as no surprise that hope is stamped all over the scriptures. The history of salvation opens with God making a promise to Abraham. Here we hear God's pledge to be active in Abraham's future.

> Go from country and your kindred and your father's house to the land that I will show you. I will make of you a great nation, and I will bless you, and make your name great, so that you will be a blessing. I will bless those who bless you, and the one who curses you I will curse; and in you all the families of the earth shall be blessed. (Gen 12: 1–3)

First, God commands Abraham, but note what a strange thing it is: I want you to leave home and go someplace, but I'm not going to tell you where yet. Astonishingly Abraham sets out!

But most of the passage is given over to promise. Here it contains the following: you will be a great nation, I will bless you, your name will be great, you will be a blessing, I will protect you, and through you all of humanity will find God's blessing. What an stunning set of promises this is! Note the importance, please, of the idea of promise. God will be active in Abraham's affairs in such a way that Abraham's future will be full of divine blessings. Promise always stands as the basis for hope. Abraham found the courage to leave it all behind and step into a God-formed future exactly because he had hope. Abraham could declare to himself: my destiny is good, because God has said so.

In these three short verses lay before us some of the major themes of the Bible. God cares enough about humanity to roll up God's sleeves and get involved in our world. God always seeks to bless. God calls forth hope as we face the future, and that future is based on divine promises. But the promises of God are seldom instantaneous, and, therefore, patience becomes a corollary virtue to hope. The psalmist writing many centuries after Abraham has learned the lesson of the great patriarch. He writes, "I wait for the LORD, my soul waits, and in his word I hope . . . O Israel, hope in the LORD! For with the LORD there is steadfast love, and with him is great power to redeem." (Ps 130: 3, 7)

The death and resurrection of Jesus Christ both sharpens and complicates the idea of hope. The resurrection shouts out the victory of God over all things in heaven and earth, and that includes even the strongest of humanity's enemies, death. Hope finds its firmest ground in God raising Jesus from the dead.

I have asked that the following be read at my funeral.

> It is Christ Jesus who died, yes, who was raised, who indeed intercedes for you. Who will separate us from the love of Christ? . . . For I am convinced that neither death, nor life, nor angels,

nor rulers not things present, nor things to come, nor powers, nor height, nor depth, nor anything else in all creation, will be able to separate from the love of God in Christ Jesus our Lord. (Rom 8: 34–35, 38–39)

The traditional symbol for hope is an anchor, and Christians anchor their hope on the promise of the resurrection we will share with our loving Lord.

We began with the beginning of the story of Abraham. We turn now to an incident from the ministry of Jesus. He goes to the little town of Nain, and as he approaches the gate there he encounters a funeral procession. The body of a young man is being carried out; near by is his mother, and Jesus learns that the man is the only son of the woman, who is a widow. Jesus is moved with compassion and tells the women not to weep. He goes to the bier, touches the body, and speaks to it: Young man, I say get up. And, wonder of wonders, the once-dead man sits up and begins to talk. The town is seized with awe and fear, and they sense that God has been active among them. And word of the event spreads throughout the area. You can find the exact text in Luke 7: 11–17.

In the story we know almost without thinking that a dead person has no future and that we cannot have any hope for him. But his mother also with in a dire state. She has lost her only son and is also a widow; she is without anyone to support her, and her future is bleak, indeed.

Into this despairing situation steps Jesus. Note he is moved with compassion for the woman and gives her an odd command: stop crying. Next Jesus touches the dead man, and in that act he has according to the ritual law of his people made himself unclean and unacceptable to God. That is, Jesus has fully immersed himself into the hopelessness of the situation and has made it his own.

But his word to the man creates life, and the young man lives and returns to his mother.

The presence of Jesus brings hope into a hopeless place. His word breaks the grip and death and life returns to the young man. This episode anticipates what is to come, namely, the dead young man will be Jesus himself, who will be raised to life beyond death by God. The people of Nain interpret this Easter-like event done in their midst: "God has looked favorably on (literally, has visited) his people." The presence of God promises life and thereby always creates hope.

DISCUSSION QUESTIONS

First, discuss the difference between hope and optimism.

Second, what are some of the anxious places in your life that need the promise of hope?

Third, discuss the manner in which our baptism into Christ's death and resurrection engenders hope.

Fourth, how can your church be an agent of God's hope in your community?

chapter 18

Incarnation
God Made Flesh

IN THE FIRST CHURCH I served we had a good and active Sunday School. In the course of a year, the teachers worked at helping the kids meet and love Jesus. Every year an important event happened on the Sunday before Christmas. The usual coffee hour was turned into a Sunday School event that was, in fact, a birthday party for Jesus. It always included a big cake with the words "Happy Birthday Jesus!" written across the top.

This is perfectly suitable for children, but adults need to go several layers deeper. What we celebrate at Christmas is the incarnation, a word that means simply "in the flesh." God took on human form, indeed, became fully human, and dwelled among us in the person of Jesus, son of Mary. The fact is we do not know the actual date of Jesus' birth, but the church selected December 25 as a time to lift up the great miracle of the incarnation.

From the outset we must acknowledge that we cannot explain the workings of the incarnation. It is simply a great yet wondrous mystery. What we can say is that the people who encountered and knew Jesus sensed that to be with him was like being in the divine presence. They saw his signs and miracles and recognized in them the hand of God. And his resurrection served as the great mark of authenticity of his incarnation.

The first several centuries of the church saw bishops and theologians putting their minds to work on probing the incarnation and its implications, and they used the best categories of Greek philosophy as their mode of thought. The results are found in the ancient creeds of the church, preeminently the Nicene Creed.

But I have to admit that my familiarity with Greek philosophy comes from a Philosophy 101 class taken many decades ago and a couple of books read since. I am in no position to attempt a careful interpretation of the proceedings of those ancient meetings. But I do have a Bible. And my reading, study and praying with the Bible has convinced me that that we can make our way into the "inside" of the incarnation by way of several biblical narratives.

Probably what comes to mind first is Luke 2: 1-20, what we usually call the Christmas story. This tells us about Jesus' birth in a stable, shepherds in the fields, and the announcement of his birth by an angel. What we learn from the angel comes in the form of three titles bestowed on Jesus: "To you is born this day in the city of David a Savior, who is the Messiah, the Lord." (v. 11) These function as titles of power; savior and lord were applied to the Roman emperor, and the messiah was the one who would restore Israel to the glory it held in the golden age of Kings David and Solomon. Hints of heaven hover around these terms, but this is not incarnation.

We need to turn, rather, to the story of the annunciation, which you can find in Luke 1: 26-38. Here is a quick summary.

- We meet Mary, a young woman probably about fourteen or fifteen and still living with her parents.
- Mary is engaged to Joseph and is a virgin.
- The archangel Gabriel appears to Mary. He greets her and tells her God is with her.
- She is perplexed, wondering what this means.
- Gabriel explains. Do not fear, he tells her, because she has found favor with God. He says she will conceive and bear a son whom she will name Jesus.
- Then Gabriel describes her son: he will be great, called the Son of God, the throne of his ancestor David will be given him by God, he will reign over the people of God, and his kingdom will have no end.
- Mary is further perplexed, noting that she is a virgin.
- Gabriel explains: the Holy Spirit will overshadow you and, therefore, the child will be holy and will be the Son of God. As proof, he points

INCARNATION

to Mary's barren relative Elizabeth, who has miraculously become pregnant.
- Gabriel add that with God nothing is impossible.
- Then comes Mary's famous reply: Here I am, God's servant. Let it be as you have said.

Again you see titles are heaped on Jesus, and again hints of the divine linger around all of them. He will be God's messiah, and his given name suggests that he will be the savior. But incarnational ideas appear with the description of the Holy Spirit overshadowing Mary. I believe we are to conclude that Jesus will be human from his mother Mary and divine from the presence of God's Spirit. Again, we have entered the realm of mystery, but I find that this beautiful story helps me sense the reality of incarnation in a way that moves me beyond the intellectual level.

The New Testament passage that takes us to the greatest depths is John chapter one. I think we should think of this as a grand and cosmic poem, and, in fact, some translations print it in poem form. Jesus' is entitled the Word; in Greek it is *Logos*. It's a complex word. It suggests the structure of God's mind, the logic by which God think. It also implies God's self-disclosure, the word God wishes to speak. And finally, in context it stands as God's address to the world, what God has on God's mind and wishes to disclose. Jesus is that Word.

The poem comes to a climax with these words. "And the Word became flesh and lived among us, and we have seen his glory, the glory as of a father's only son, full of grace and truth." (John 1: 14) I know of no more profound or helpful statement of incarnation than that.

What might we conclude from this quick skip through some Bible stories? First, God cared enough to come among us. When I was in college I communicated with my parents by letter, and they replied in the same way. Part of our arrangement was that I would send at least a post card every week. But I well remember one day a knock on the door and there were my father and my brother. It's one thing to get mail, but it's quite another to get a visit. The first is a statement of care, but the later involves effort and commitment. God had made a covenant with the people of Israel, and God was present in the Law and the prophets. But in the arrival of the Word made flesh we move into a new dimension of relationship.

Second, God knows us from the inside out. For example, we can be with people when they are sick, we can observe what they endure, and we can comfort them. But it changes when we are sick, when we know illness from personal experience. I have been blessed by God with good health, and it can be easy for me to deal with the sick in a surface way. At that moment I can recall my five days in the hospital with a bad case of flu; in a way, that we a blessing that now allows me to understanding being ill from the inside out. Because of the incarnation God knows us in the most intimate sense.

Three, in the incarnation God honors and dignifies the material world. I had a professor who once told us that all of western philosophy is simply a footnote to Plato. It's an exaggeration that points to a truth. Part of Plato's thinking was that the material world was tainted, but that world of the mind and spirit were pure and served as direct links with the divine. If we could just tame our bodies and train our minds we would be in touch with the ideal world of the divine. These ideas have been whispered in the back hallways of the church for centuries. But the incarnation says that the material world, too, is beloved of God, and, in fact, is used by God to do God's mission. Jesus, fully a human being with body, feelings, desires, hungers, and pains, is God's definitive self-revelation.

Finally, the incarnation empowers a crisp vision of our faith. We are not primarily about ideas, philosophy, rules, meditation techniques, or experience. To be sure, we do use ideas and philosophy, we have rules, we possess a rich store of wisdom about meditation, and experience and feeling are a part of our lives. But our basic focus is a person, Jesus Christ, son of Mary. He is the Word made flesh, God incarnate, the one who united heaven and earth, the person who draws all humanity into one.

More than twenty-five years ago I was able to make a pilgrimage to the Holy Land. I had read the Bible thoroughly and had heard the stories from early childhood on. I believed that Jesus inhabited my mind and my imagination. But then I went to Israel. I still recall climbing a set of stone steps in Jerusalem, and at the top our guide turned to us and said, "Jesus himself certainly climbed those very steps." Cold chills ran through me. It became really real. Jesus the incarnation of God, really real.

DISCUSSION QUESTIONS;

First, define incarnation in your own words.

INCARNATION

Second, is there a Bible story about Jesus that especially helps you sense the truth of the incarnation?

Three, what aspects of Jesus' humanity mean the most to you?

Four, if God could be incarnate in Jesus, Jesus could be incarnate in the bread and wine of the Eucharist. Do you agree? Is so, why?

chapter 19

Jesus
What's in a Name?

SOME OF US REMEMBER John Lennon declaring that he was more famous than Jesus. That happened many years ago, but I sometimes wonder what he was trying to say. At least part of his intent was to bolster his ego by declaring that he outpaced the most famous person he could think of. I suspect he was wrong. I think Jesus still holds the top spot.

But fame and celebrity are not the issues, are they? His fame rests on who he was and what he accomplished. Those represent the issues I wish to explore.

Sometimes a great importance lies in a person's name, especially in holy scripture. Jesus serves as a case in point. His name means "God will save" in Aramaic, the common language of Jesus and those among whom he lived. In Luke 1: 31 we hear that the archangel Gabriel tell Mary that she must name him Jesus. His name sums up his life and mission.

Today we often call him "Jesus Christ" as if Christ is part of his name. That word is a title, not a name. In Greek it means "anointed one" and the Hebrew form of it is Messiah. In his own day he was known as Jesus of Nazareth or Jesus son of Joseph. Early Christians called him Jesus the Christ, and soon that was abbreviated to the form commonly used today. But his proper name was "God will save," Jesus.

Beginning in the eighteenth century some scholars, particularly in Germany, raised the issue of Jesus' historical identity. They made a distinction between the Jesus of faith whom we know through the gospels and the

Jesus of history. Moreover they tended to be skeptical of much of the material in the Bible. Many, for instance, questioned any supernatural narratives such as the miracle stories and the resurrection. One joke says that one of these famous scholars was working at his desk when a colleague arrives and excitedly tells him that the bones of Jesus have been discovered, to which the scholar replies, "You mean he actually existed?"

Today virtually no one would question that Jesus lived. His person and work are recorded in the gospels, of course, but are also mentioned by Josephus, Tacitus, Suetonius and Pliny, all prominent and non-Christian Roman writers. Jesus was likely born in the spring of 4 BC; in spring the shepherds kept watch over their flocks by night as Luke 2 tells us. His public ministry likely began in 27 AD, and he died on the fourteenth or fifteenth of the Jewish month of Nisan in 30 AD; in our calendar that day is April 7.

We can discover a great deal about who Jesus is by focusing on the four big events in his life: his birth, baptism, death, and resurrection. Naturally we begin with his birth. The familiar story of his birth can be found in Luke 2. In that story heaven and earth are pulled together and united. We meet his parents Mary and Joseph as well as shepherds, an innkeeper, the Roman emperor, and likely a midwife and curious onlookers. But heaven is involved in the form of angels who declare a message from God and sing a song of praise. All this finds in focus on the tiny one sleeping in a manger.

You remember that the angel in the proclamation to the shepherds gives three titles to Jesus: Savior, Christ, and Lord. A subversive element finds expression here in as much as Savior and Lord were titles for the emperor, titles that were engraved on coins and expressed the god-like character of the emperor. Messiah, as noted above, is a Jewish term, and was a "hot" term for the people of Palestine. Many, but not all, Jewish people believed that the messiah would be a descendent of the great King David, who led the tribes of Israel into its golden age around 1000 BC. Furthermore, they hoped that the messiah would reestablish the kingdom of Israel by defeating the Roman oppressors and then lead the people into a new golden age. In other words they hoped for a dynamic political and military leader. But here was little Jesus, born out back in a stable, the son of poor people, and honored by a raggedy band of shepherds.

We can hardly ignore the paradoxical elements in Jesus' beginnings. Once again God shows that surprise and mystery characterize the way God works among human beings. The biblical narrative above all else invites us to keep our eye on this child, because God clearly is initiating a new thing, a new relationship, a new covenant with humanity through Jesus.

After his birth we leap forward about twelve years to hear the story of Jesus as a child holding discussions with the official teachers of the Jewish people. This foreshadows Jesus' work as a teacher. But next we leap ago across the years to his encounter with one of the oddest persons in the Bible, John the Baptist. John has taken on the role of a prophet even to the point of dressing like Elijah, one of Israel's first and greatest spokespersons for God. John proclaims that God is about to act in a decisive way, and that people must prepare for that event by being baptized as a sign of their repentance, their desire to set things right with God. And one day Jesus presents himself to John for baptism.

All four gospels contain accounts of Jesus' baptism (Matt 3: 13–17, Mark 1: 9–11, Luke 3: 21–22, John 1: 31–34) Each has its unique characteristics, but the major elements of the story are clear. Three factors stand foremost. The divine voice speaks as Jesus is baptized and names him as Son of God. Second, he is declared to be the beloved of God, and, finally, the Holy Spirit descends on Jesus. The title of Son was commonly used for the ruler of God's people; in Jesus's case this hinted at his messiahship, but as we will see he will not be a king in a political sense. The title of "beloved" has many antecedents in the Old Testament: the son Abraham almost sacrificsd to God in Genesis, the suffering servant of Isaiah, and even the whole people of God. Any of these deserves more treatment that we can give here, but all refer to specially chosen people who will accomplish God's mission in significant ways. And in all cases the Holy Spirit is bestowed. This says that the fullness of God now dwells in Jesus and will empower him to do God's work.

Jesus' identity, mission, and empowerment are bestowed on him directly by God through the baptism of John. Afterward, Jesus goes into the wilderness for a forty day retreat during which his identity will be tested by the Evil One. And then Jesus moves into the public sphere.

The gospel of Mark gives us a summary of Jesus' proclamation, which proclamation, in turn, interprets his actions. "Jesus came to Galilee, proclaiming the good news of God, saying 'The time is fulfilled, and the kingdom of God has come near; repent, and believe in the good news." (Mark 1. 14–15) Note the four points of his preaching:

- the time is fulfilled, that is, we have arrived at the moment God has been planning throughout the ages;

- the Kingdom is at hand, that is, that reality in which God's will is done is now present in the person of Jesus;
- repent, that is, change your direction in life and orient your thoughts, actions, and will toward God; and
- believe the good news, that is, put your trust in what God is doing in Jesus.

When we take that essential message and compare it with Jesus' activity we can make conclusions about how the Kingdom of God looks and operates. Jesus healed the sick, cast out demons, forgave sinners, accepted outcasts, feed the hungry, and challenged the rich and powerful. Thus, when God is in charge we look for health, holiness, forgiveness, acceptance, the basic of life, and justice.

All four gospels narrate the death of Jesus in a laconic, no-nonsense way. They make no appeals to emotion or sentiment. Jesus had called into question the whole Temple system and the leaders who controlled and profited from that system. When he overturned the tables of the money changers (in John 2, for example) he had, in effect, declared war on the money-making schemes of the leaders. In order to make atonement for your sins by means of the sacrificial system detailed in the Old Testament you had to deal with exchanging common currency for Temple coins, and you then had to purchase the sheep or doves from merchants. All of this was set up to profit the leaders. Furthermore, Jesus challenged the teachings and the authority of the leaders. After a certain point those leaders plotted to take Jesus' life. The end came quickly and his death was ignominious in every way. To explore the meaning of his death, look at the chapters on the cross and on sacrifice.

With the resurrection of Jesus we reach the climax of his story and the very center of our faith. Paul tell us what is at stake here: "If Christ has not ben raised, your faith is futile and you are still in your sins . . . But in fact Christ has been raised from the dead, the first fruits of those who have died." (1 Cor 15: 17, 20) I have written a chapter on resurrection in this book, and I ask you to refer to it for more details. But briefly, the resurrection accomplishes three things. First, it signals God's approval of Jesus, especially his death. It is God's seal of approval for what was accomplished by our Lord on the cross.

Second, the resurrection demonstrates God's victory over death and all that separates us from God. In as much as God was able to raise Jesus from the dead, we see that nothing can stand in the way of God's life and love. One of the most used ancient Christian symbols was the four Greek letters *NIKE*, victory.

Three, the resurrection assures us that we can look to the future with hope. When we share in Jesus' resurrection by virtue of our baptism we can be certain that God will make something good and worthy out of anything and all things that happen to us.

In general, then, we can declare that if you want to know God you need to be encountered by Jesus Christ. He is our window into the very heart of God. One early Christian writer notes that Jesus is the image of God. (Col 1: 15) The word for image in Greek is icon. We know icons today as painted images that serve as windows in the Kingdom of God. Later he adds, "For in him the fullness of God was pleased to dwell, and through him God was pleased to reconcile to himself all things . . . by making peace through the blood of the cross." (Col 1: 19–20)

When I receive an invitation to an event I often find "r.s.v.p." written at the bottom. It's an acronym for the French phrase "respond, if you please." When we are encountered by Jesus we always find ourselves placed at a point of decision. As I hope you sense dealing with Jesus is a matter of life and death. And he always says to us, "Respond, if you please."

The way we step into the new reality opened for us by the incarnation, death, and resurrection of Jesus is Holy Baptism. From the earliest days of the church as described in the New Testament book of the Acts of the Apostles, baptism is the means by which God unites us to Christ, but it always stands as an act of commitment to Jesus.

The baptismal liturgy in my own Episcopal Church delineates this clearly. When a person presents her and himself for baptism, they are asked by the priest to renounce three factors: first, Satan and all the spiritual forces aligned with him; second, all the evil powers that corrupt and destroy God's creatures; and three, all the sinful desires that draw one away from loving God.

Then the baptismal candidate is asked to make three affirmations. First, do you turn and accept Jesus Christ as your Savior; two, do you put your whole trust in him; and do you promise to follow and obey him? Only then can the baptism proceed.

These renunciations and affirmations ask, and even demand, that at baptism the candidate will set forth on a life seriously dedicated to obedience to Christ. This represents an r.s.v.p. of the highest order.

JESUS

I have served as a bishop for over fifteen years, and as you might expect my views about living in Christ have changed over that time, and I hope they have changed in the direction of more wisdom and maturity. One of those turning points for me came during a discussion with members of a vestry of one of my churches. They were troubled by several developments in the life of the congregation, and were seeking clearer direction from me. Suddenly it occurred to me to ask simply, "Do you love Jesus." I really do believe that it can be as simple as that. Do you love Jesus? From my perspective how could we not love him in the light of his blazing love for us?

The psalmist says it best. "Whom have I in heaven but you? and having you I desire nothing upon earth." (Ps 73: 25, Book of Common Prayer translation, p. 688)

DISCUSSION QUESTIONS

First, who is Jesus for you?

Two, if you were to make a commitment or recommitment to Christ today, what form would that take?

Three, In his preaching Jesus asked for repentence? What would that look like for you?

Four, the gospels contain many stories about Jesus driving out demons? How do you react to that? Do you think demons are active spiritual forces? If so, how do they operate?

chapter 20

Justification
Getting Right with God

Recently I walked out the back door of the cathedral in Helena when a stranger approached me. He had tattered clothes and a skinny dog followed him, and I jumped to the conclusion that he was going to beg for money. He, however, asked who owned the red SUV, and I replied that it was mine. "I nicked it," he said. Note my first response: "I parked within the lines." I wanted to justify myself; I wanted to state that I was not to blame. The stranger went on to apologize many times over. Together we inspected the nick, which was frankly almost too small to see. When he departed I found myself impressed with his scrupulous honest and ashamed of my defensiveness.

The desire to justify ourselves seems a basic part of human nature, does it not? We all want to demonstrate that we are in the right.

I can describe how this dynamic works in my life. Perhaps you will be able to recognize yourself in my experience. So, if I am in the wrong, then I need to apologize. That is, I need to make a public statement that I erred in some way. And I hate to apologize, because I feel as if I am diminished, that I, in fact, die a little in my deepest sense of self. So, I try to find a way to set what I have done within a frame of acceptable behavior. I nicked your car, but you should understand that my vehicle was designed with poor sight lines. I shouted at you, but you should know that I grew up in a home where I was shouted at constantly. And so it goes.

JUSTIFICATION

If we were honest we would have to admit that justifying ourselves would be nearly a full-time job. I seem to stumble from mistake to error to revenge to anger and back again.

The Book of Common Prayer used in my church helps me get to the heart of the matter. Part of the most commonly recited prayer of confession reads, "We have not loved [God] with our whole heart; we have not loved our neighbors as ourselves." (p. 360) For the baptized this represents a major fissure in our lives. Listen to Jesus in his response to the Sadducees, who asked him which commandment is the great. He said, "'You shall love the Lord your God with all your heart, and with all your soul, and with all your mind.' This is the greatest and first commandment. And a second is like it: 'You shall love your neighbor as yourself.' On these two commandments hang all the law and the prophets." (Matt 22: 37–40) What person can honestly claim never to have violated these? What person can claim to have gotten through a day without breaking them?

We cannot stand justified before God. From top to bottom we fail often to love God and neighbor. The Episcopal Diocese of Ohio has distributed a bumper sticker, one of which I have posted on my truck. It reads, "Love God. Love neighbor. Change the world." At some level we recognize that Jesus' command is not mere moralism, but, in fact, represents what our world needs most. We know that self-sacrificing love, the sort of love demonstrated by Jesus on the cross, resonates with our deepest needs and would transform the world if we could practice it.

The good news can be declared in many ways. Here is one powerful way: God has chosen and has acted to justify us. We cannot do it for ourselves, but God can. At root the Bible reveals a God who longs to be in loving relationship with humanity, and because of that God acts to make it happen. In classic language God justifies sinners.

This represents God's will in the Old Testament no less than in the New. For example, consider Psalm 25. "All the paths of the LORD are steadfast love and faithfulness, for those who keep his covenant and his decrees." (v. 10) On the basis of that the psalmist can pray, "My eyes are ever toward the LORD, for he will pluck my feet out of the net. Turn to me and be gracious to me, for I am lonely and afflicted. Relieve the troubles of my heart, and bring me out of my distress. Consider my affliction and my trouble, and forgive all my sins." (vss. 15–18) Because of God's nature we can expect God's grace and favor to be active in our lives.

The Language of Love

Probably the idea of a justifying God finds its most prominent place in the writings of Paul. He uses the term to describe God's decision to accept us, and this comes into effect through Jesus. He uses rather technical language, but simply put he proclaims that if we trust the God revealed in Jesus God's grace will be active in our lives. We will stand justified before God.

Those who trust God "are now justified by his grace a a gift, through the redemption that I in Christ Jesus, whom God put forward as a sacrifice of atonement by his blood, effective through faith. He did this show his righteousness." (Rom 3: 24–25) As I said, Paul wraps this thoughts in the technical language of cultic sacrifice. I recommend the article on sacrifice elsewhere in this book.

Let me attempt a summary. In Jesus we perceive God standing with humanity, and on the cross we witness God embracing and making God's own all the awful things that sap away our lives, including the fact of death itself. All God wants from us is to trust that God accepts us as we are, and in doing that we can enter into God's presence fully accepted and valued. That is justification.

Terms associated with justification are righteousness and justice. But in scripture they are not always used in the ordinary sense of doing the right things and being fair. Rather they are qualities of God, and they are turned upside-down from their usual usage. For God the right and just thing to do is to justify people, that is, to accept them as they are. This happens because God's basic nature is love.

Perhaps the classic story can be found in John 8: 1–11, the episode of the woman caught in adultery. The scribes and Pharisees drag before Jesus a woman caught in the act of committing adultery. I myself wonder what subterfuge they used to catch the woman in the act, and I further wonder why they did not present also the man involved. The plot thickens when we remember that the Pharisees formed a lay renewal movement within Judaism; they tended to be rather well-off people with an intense commitment to keeping the Law as found in the Old Testament. The scribes were the experts in the Law; we might call them biblical scholars. My sense, and perhaps you will not agree, is that they are rather enjoying putting a sinner on display while congratulating themselves on not being adulterers. They remind Jesus that the Law commands the woman to be stoned to death, and they ask for his response. They believe they have put Jesus between the proverbial rock and hard place. This may indicate they knew of Jesus' compassion for sinners, and wanted to force his hand. Is it compassion, or is it the Law? Famously Jesus bends down and writes in the sand. The scribes and Pharisees keep pressing Jesus, and he stands and says, "Let anyone among you who is without sin be the first to throw a stone at her." (vs. 7) And he returns to writing, but the antagonists go away beginning with the eldest among the group. Jesus looks up and asks the woman where her accusers have gone. "'Has no one condemned you?' She said, 'No one, sir.' And Jesus said, 'Neither do I condemn you. Go your way, and from now one do not sin again.'" (vss. 10–11)

I find this to be an amazing story, rich in both detail and significance. But for our purposes note that no one stands guiltless before God. I suspect the eldest in the group left first out of a sense that he stood accused before God, if not for adultery then for a host of other things over the course of his long life. Also, most of all note that Jesus does not condemn. The woman is free to go, commanded only to clean up her life in the future. It's a story that acts out justification.

We stand justified. But how do we live into that new reality? Suppose that on a cold, gray winter day you received notice that you had won a free ocean cruise on a luxury liner. You sign up to collect your trip, you pack, and you arrive at port. Think about the differences that trip would make in your life. You would be infused with a sense of happiness and anticipation. You would get out your summer clothes and probably buy some new things for the cruise. On the trip you would enjoy gourmet food, new friends, and evening entertainment. You would, in fact, be living in a different reality, the cruise reality, and you would eagerly line into it.

By virtue of our baptism into Christ we have become part of a new reality. That new state of living allows us to live into the unbreakable covenant God has initiated for us. We can struggle with that relationship and we can even reject it, but for God it is immutable and eternal. Is it possible for us to digest this and make it a part of our imagination and nature? We can, and we should. As justified person we can build out lives on the sure sense that before God we are OK. We and trust that God will fulfill for us God's purpose for us and for the church.

My wife had a relative who would not drive his car over bridges. In some way he did not trust the bridge to deliver him to the other side. Most of us simply trust the bridges we use. What if our trust in the reliability of the God who justifies us were as basic as our trust in bridges?

Second, we do not need to get caught in the net of scrupulosity. One of my past spiritual directors, a wonderfully compassionate Jesuit priest, once told me that he found this to be a common spiritual issue. It consists of compulsion about one's sins, mistakes, and errors. It seeks only what we have done wrong or failed to do, and cannot move on to the good news that God in Christ justifies people even when their lives have become a web of error and sin. This, in turn, often seems to make brittle and harsh people, people fascinated by their own sin and overly concerned about the failures of others. There simply is no need for this attitude. God knows that we are fragile, struggling, often sinful people, and the death and resurrection of Christ demonstrate that God nevertheless accepts us.

Third, because we are justified and are aware of both the divine and human dynamics behind that, we live with the constant call of repentance. I had another spiritual director, a monk in The Episcopal Church, who became angry with me while I was in the process of confession. "It's the same old sins all the time," he said. I perceived his comments as a call to make some forward movement in my life in terms of developing greater holiness. I was stuck in a rut of sin, and I learned then that it was time to reorient my life and apply some discipline to myself. God accepts us as we are, but God never desires that we simply stay where we are. I believe it was the master pianist Arthur Rubenstein who had a saying about the necessity of practice. "If I don't practice one day, I can tell. If I do not practice two days, my friends can tell. If I don't practice three days, everyone can tell." We as justified people are call to the constant and daily spiritual discipline of repentance and holiness.

It was my grandmother who taught me this simple definition of justification. It means: just as if I had never sinned. So it is.

DISCUSSION QUESTIONS

First, for God the right and just thing to do is the justify sinners. Does this seem fair to you? Should we not be held accountable for our actions? How would you respond to these issues?

Two, do you think we can or should adopt God's justifying attitude toward others?

Three, how would you explain justification to someone who had never heard of the concept?

chapter 21

Love
All We Need Is Love

I SOMETIMES MEANDER MY way through YouTube looking for little tidbits that delight or interest me. One evening I came across a black-and-white film of one of my favorite singers, Ella Fitzgerald. She was making magic with the McHugh and Fields classic "I Can't Give You Anything But Love." Then she sang it in the style of Billie Holiday and next like Louie Armstrong. Her performance swept me away. Part of her genius consisted in the ability to get behind the words and project something of he depth of the song. "I can't give you anything but love, baby. That's the only thing I've plenty of, baby." I had the sense that Ella believed shes had arrived at one of life's bottom lines in the words of that song.

Our culture celebrates love. We want it. Indeed, we need it. Songs and movies, essays and sermons all proclaim that to be truth. The twentieth-century theologian Paul Tillich believed that we all have three great issues that drive our lives. How can I deal with my guilt and failure? Does my life have meaning and purpose? How do I face death? I would say that below these three questions lies the deepest need of all. Am I lovable? Can anyone know me thoroughly and love me anyway? Would anyone stand by me through thick and thin? Can I find love?

Maybe because the word carries such weighty importance we tend to use it frequently and on many occasions. So we say that we love chocolate or the Los Angeles Dodgers. We speak of love of our pets as well as love of our country. And surely we can list people we love. Maybe you sense that the word shifts meaning often.

Maybe we need more words, more terms to assist us in our analysis of love. The Greek language has a number of names for the general concept of love, and they can help us in our understanding. First is *eros*. We know it, of course, is our English term erotic. Eros consists of the desire to possess and enjoy. We find it in our phrase "I love chocolate." This sort of love suggests a subject-object relationship, and is, therefore, basically egocentric. I want that person or thing because it will enable my pleasure. The blatant form of erotic love crops up in pornography, which thrives on using someone for the purposes of gratification only. Note carefully that *eros* is not found in the New Testament, even though it may be the most common meaning of the love in our society.

In 1682 William Penn founded a city at the confluence of the Delaware and Schuylkill Rivers. He envisioned it as an experiment in social friendship, hardly a surprise for a member of the Society of Friends. He called it Philadelphia. The Greek term is *phileo*. It suggests friendship and social affection. The phrase "I just love my circle of friends" encapsulates this sort of love.

Stergo connotes the love of family. The affection that binds together siblings stands as an instance.

But now we arrive at the heart of the matter. What is translated as "love" in many passages of the New Testament is the Greek term *agape*. Before the rise of the church the term was not commonly used but became a precious word for Christians. Probably the most famous passage in the New Testament makes use of this word: "God so loved the world that he gave is only Son, so that everyone who believes in him may not perish by may have eternal life." (John 3: 16) It suggests unselfish concern for others, and finds it grounding in an "I-Thou" relationship. Notice in the John passage that the words "love" and "give" occur as near synonyms.

We can make three statements that unpack *agape* for us. First, it focuses on others, not self. Second, it seeks the good for the other. Indeed, it desires God's blessings for the other. Third, it sets self aside in order to accomplish that goal, even to the point of sacrifice of one's self.

As a child it filled me with pride to know that my uncle was part of the honor guard at Tomb of the Unknown Soldier. We all revere that anonymous person because he gave the last and full measure of himself for the sake of the country. This represented an act of *agape* for his native land.

Jesus raises the concept of *agape* love to its highest level as can be seen in his death on the cross. This applies to the breadth of divine love. As noted in the chapter on "catholic" the love of God is large enough to envelope all people at all times in all places. There is a sense in which this belies the concepts of particularity or context; God's *agape* takes in every circumstance.

This sort of love, furthermore, is bottomless. No circumstance is too painful or horrible for God's love. At the cross humanity threw at Jesus just about every awful thing that could happen, yet he did not flinch at embracing it. He did not take vengeance or curse his persecutors. He made it all his own. He set aside self to the ultimate degree in order to set humanity free.

And divine love cannot be defeated. This must certainly be one of the points of the resurrection. Not even death, the one thing no one can escape or conquer, is exempt from the power of God's self-giving love. It is deathless. It conquers all.

And this love reveals the heart of God. "God is love. God's love was revealed among us in this way: God sent his only Son into the world so that we might live through him." (1 John 4: 8b–9) At the heart of life, at the heart of the universe stands love.

There is a story that says someone asked Karl Barth, the twentieth-century Swiss theologian, to summarize his work. He replied, "Jesus loves me this I know for the Bible tells me so." I do not want to suggest that God's sacrificial love is soft, childish, or sentimental, but I do want to declare that divine love epitomizes the good news of Jesus Christ. This love represents the power of the resurrection, the power to change hard hearts and open closed minds. This power sustains people in the most difficult of circumstances. This power changes the course of history and give human life a grand and great purpose.

And the church is called to live in and by the power of this love. Our role as Christians is not to be nice, middle class Americans. Rather, we have been empowered by this love to sacrifice for the sake of others, to share the good news, to overcome all the barriers that divide us, and to serve all in need. The story of the church includes chapters where Christians are called to sacrifice life itself. This goes on today in the Middle East. We may not be asked to give up life itself for the sake of God's love, but surely all are called to sacrifice time, talent, and treasure to carry on the ministry of our Lord.

The last congregation I served worked with other churches in the community to feed people on Sundays. We had discovered that all the other feeding programs ceased to operate on Sunday, so we stepped into that gap.

We used the kitchen and assembly room of a church in the midst of the most distressed part of the city. One Sunday I was there and noted a particularly unpleasant smell. "What is that?" I asked. The vicar of the church replied, "That is the smell of poverty." I am especially adverse to unpleasant odors, and my every impulse was to exit the room. I grant you that this is a small thing, but my little sacrifice that day was to stay and help prepare a good meal.

Many years ago I called on a elderly couple. The woman was standing at the kitchen counter putting together a recipe. The cook book was open, and various ingredients and measuring cups were neatly spread out on the counter. The husband was standing directly behind his wife, and he said to me, "She's cooking." I knew that she was nearly completely blind, but he would hand her ingredients and coach her along. A beautiful smile graced her face.

God works with us in a similar way. He shapes our world and lives by *agape*. And now it is our turn to go and do likewise.

DISCUSSION QUESTIONS

First, please state your own definition of divine love.

Second, when and where has that been present and active in your life?

Three, write a short prayer of thanksgiving for God's love.

Four, consider what you can give in grateful response to God's love.

chapter 22

Mystery

Into the Depths of God

I LOVE TO VISIT book stores, and when in one the first place I go to is the mystery section. I almost always have one of these in my stack of active books. You know the formula for this sort of novel: a crime is committed, the protagonist works at finding and interpreting clues, and at the end the villain is revealed and justice prevails.

We also use the word mystery to connote something beyond our knowing. For instance, how many stars does the universe contain? Any answer to that is at best a guesstimate.

But in scripture "mystery" is not used in either of these ways. In thinking about God we must admit that God's workings are so rich and full that we cannot take it all in nor can we get to the bottom of it. But none of that should be taken to suggest that we cannot know something about the ways of God; we can have some understanding, even though it may be partial.

The New Testament makes use of "mystery" in this last sense. The apostle Paul, for instance, plays with the word in wonderful ways. At one point he writes that he wants his churches to "have all the riches of assured understanding and have the knowledge of God's mystery, that is, Christ himself, in whom are hidden all the treasures of wisdom and knowledge." (Colossians 2: 2–3) Note that he hopes Christians will have knowledge of and assurance about God' great mystery. That, of course, has an element of paradox about it, and I think it contains a touch of humor as well. And then note that Christ himself constitutes the mystery of God. He reveals the fulness of God and at the same time presents us with the depths of God beyond our capability to understand.

What can we say as we who seek to follow Jesus by living into the mystery of God? What should we expect? First, exactly because we are dealing with God we should expect to encounter mystery at every turn. God is by definition beyond our understanding. If we could grasp fully God, then God would hardly qualify as God. This situation suggests that we should not overestimate our human intellectual abilities.

The French philosopher Descartes wrote "I think, therefore I am." This posits our rationality as the basis for our humanity. We tend to measure all things against our ability to measure, analyze, study, and categorize it. Moreover, we tend to dismiss anything we cannot grasp. Given this assumption God has not fared well in the modern mind; it has been easy to dismiss the whole category of the supernatural as unnecessary, if not non-existent. I myself, however, do not want to reduce my humanity to my ability to carry out rational thought. My ability to be in relationship, to make commitments, to exercise my will, to be moved by art and music, to seek God all need to be considered as part of my humanity.

If God is mystery we should also expect to encounter paradox when we think about God. A paradox consists of two contradictory statement both of which are true. Is light a wave or a particle? The impossible but true answer is: both. In our journey with God we will encounter many such statements. For instance, Christians insist that Jesus was both fully divine and fully human. That statement is contradictory yet true. God is both transcendent and imminent. Again, contradictory yet true.

Paradox can, however, be particularly difficult. A persistent question in our culture is this: if God is powerful and loving, why does God permit pain and evil in the world. I have never found a quick and convincing answer to that paradoxical puzzle. But we throw out the best answers we can find. If someone suffers from serious illness, we might say that that represents the will of God or that God is punishing for sins committed. But when we stack those replies up against what we know of God through Jesus they do not add up. Jesus healed people, not made them sick, and he forgave people rather than pronounce punishment. And in his death on the cross we perceive God in Christ accepting and embracing all the pain and grief of life. I find what I know about God comforting, helpful and hopeful, but the paradox remains.

Mystery

My wife and I have been married over forty-three years. During those decades we have been through thick and thin together. I know my wife better than any other person, and she would say the same about me. But in many ways she remains a mystery, and I cannot pretend to understand or explain everything about her. Now if that is true with her, why would I expect God to be subject to my analysis or understanding? I am content with the mystery.

DISCUSSION QUESTIONS

First, if you could ask God any question what would it be?

Second, the New Testament says that Jesus is the mystery of God revealed. What mystery do you think Jesus reveals about God?

Three, God's mystery always pushes us to know God better. What part of your relationship with God do you sense you need to explore?

chapter 23

Ordination
Leadership and Service in Christ's Church

I HAVE BEEN ORDAINED more times than most people. In my own Episcopal Church one is ordained a deacon, and then six to twelve months later one can be ordained a priest. And if elected a bishop, a third ordination takes place. Each represented a major transition in both my personal and professional life. On the wall of my office I have large certificates making each occasion, all literally signed and sealed with wax. At each event I had a deep sense that something important was taking place.

That's exactly what we want to explore in this chapter: what is taking place when a person is ordained, and why might it be important. The word itself has a Latin root meaning to appoint so as to put things in order, to arrange, or to establish. In ordination, a person is appointed to leadership in the church and invested with the power and authority to act as a leader. Moreover, exactly because this leadership occurs in the community of the church and is dedicated to God's mission the deacon, priest, and bishop are said to be in "Holy Orders."

We find the beginnings of ordination in the New Testament. Consider the incident narrated in Acts 6: 1–6. The early church performed a ministry unique in the ancient world: they took care of widows. As the church expanded the original Jewish-background Aramaic-speaking widows were joined by Gentile-background, Greek-speaking widows. The Gentile group complained to the apostles that they were being neglected in the daily distribution of food; they believed they were not getting their fair share in this meals-on-wheels program. The apostles took up the matter and put forward a proposal to the church. They said that they themselves did not want to take up this work, but suggested that seven godly person be chosen to handle it. This idea gained support, the apostles chose the seven, and then they laid hands on them with prayer. Now, this event can be considered the first ordination. The seven came to be called deacons, based on the Greek word for servant.

Note some factors in this event. The seven persons were appointed and empowered by the act of laying on of hands with prayer. This has become the standard and most important act of ordaining someone. From that point on they were assumed to take leadership in the servant work of the church, thus representing and carrying on the servant ministry that Jesus himself modeled.

As noted even to this day deacons are one of the orders of the church. They work among the poor and outcast, and they help lead the church in this important aspect of God's mission. Also note in the narrative that the apostles were seen as the chief leaders, the supervisors, of the church. This work eventually fell to a group called bishops.

That story from Acts recounts an important development for the original church in Jerusalem. Leadership was required for the Christian community to continue, and leaders were identified and set apart for that work by ordination, the laying on of hands with prayer.

As the Acts story indicates, deacons began as leaders of the ministry of service. Jesus himself came, he said, to serve, not to be served. (Mark 10: 45) Today, deacons continue to serve, and they especially do so outside the walls of the church among the poor, needy, outcasts, and the marginalized. Prison ministry, suicide prevention, and feeding programs stands as instances.

Some deacons are called to serve in this ministry for life. They are called vocational deacons. But some serve for a short period, and then are ordained as priests; these are known as transitional deacons. Thus, all priests are also deacons. In the diocese of which I am bishop, transitional deacons all work in some sort of diaconal ministry before they become a priests; in this way they have a chance to develop something of a diaconal heart even as they work as priests.

Priests are ordained to the ministry of word and sacraments. Here "word" refers not only to the Bible but also preaching, teaching, and pastoral care. They also are the ministers of the sacraments. I need to underline the fact that word and sacraments are what create and sustain the church. Through these means the Risen Christ makes himself present and available to his people. Therefore, the leadership of priests finds its basis in word and sacraments; this is the source of the authority of any priest. As corollaries to this, priests also bless, absolve sins, and take a leadership role in the governance of the church.

Bishops function as successors of the apostles. They serve as chief pastor, high priest, and leader of a diocese. They are the so-called ecclesiastical authority of the diocese, responsible for the defending the doctrine, discipline and worship of the church. They confirm and ordain. Most of what happens in a diocese occurs in some way in and through the bishop.

These are the three Holy Orders. Each is a full and distinct order, and each in its own way reflects a basic part of the ministry of Jesus. Ultimately, Jesus calls, authorizes and empowers these leaders of the church.

So far, so good. But . . . we must address now the other, crucial order, namely, the laity.

The word itself comes from Greek and means simply "the people." The persons in holy orders form a very small percentage of the membership of the church; the laity are, as my wife puts it, the regular Christians. The laity are called, authorized, and empowered for their ministry by virtue of Holy Baptism. Each lay person has a double ministry, one in the church and one in the larger world. Lay persons carry out important leadership functions; they take part in the governance of the church. In The Episcopal Church the official leaders of a congregation are the priest and elected lay people known as the vestry. Also, each lay person has been given certain skills, interests, and experiences that can be harnessed for ministry. For instance, every lay person can work in an honorable and charitable way, can witness to the presence of Christ in their lives, can support good and godly causes, and can represent our Lord in the way they order their lives. This may seem a bit mundane, but I can hardly overstate the importance of this sort of work and witness done by lay people. They form the hands and feet, eyes and ears of Christ in the world.

All baptized people have a call, a vocation, to serve and glorify Jesus Christ. In baptism we are granted the gift of the Holy Spirit, who works in and through us as well as energizes our ministries. Every Christian has skills, interests, and experiences that can be offered to God as ministry, as service to Christ and the world. I have, for example, always admired church treasurers. It's a job more complicated and time-intensive than most people imagine, and it requires a certain mindset and skills I do not have. They serve, minister, in this way. Part of the spiritual discipline each Christian needs to develop is the ability to discover and discern what the Spirit of the Risen Christ is calling you to do. And this needs to be a continuing task in as much as what one is called to often changes in the course of your life.

Furthermore, all baptized persons are called to grow and mature as disciples of Jesus. The little book of Ephesians in the New Testament lays before us the case for continual growth in Christ. This book proclaims that Jesus, crucified and risen, has overcome all barriers, so that in Christ a new, united humanity comes into being. All that divides human beings—think of race, culture, language, politics, economic status, education—has been destroyed by the cross and resurrection. And all the baptized can share in this new humanity founded by Jesus and sustained by his Spirit. In chapter four the writer notes that Christ has given grace to all disciples, and that these gifts are to be used "until all of us come to the unity of faith and of the knowledge of the Son of God, to maturity, to the measure of the full stature of Christ. We must no longer be children . . . but speaking the truth in love, we must grow up in every way into him who is the head, into Christ." (4: 13–15) Grow up. That's the command.

When my daughters were small, we made frequent trips to their doctor. Weight and height were measured, shots given, general health evaluated. My wife and I were intensely interested in these matters. They were markers of growth. Christians, too, have markers of growth. Is our relationship with Christ becoming more intimate? Are we turning over to Christ more and more aspects of our lives? Do we have a discipline of prayer and scripture study? Are we faithful in receiving communion? Would anyone who knows us suspect that we are Christians? Can we narrate our God story? The name of the game is growing up.

Very few are called to be monks. But the rest of us can be inspired by and learn from these people. The Order of St. Benedict is the original monastic group in the western church. Their motto has always been "Ora et Labora," work and pray. In fact, they collapse the two words: prayer becomes the monk's work, and his work becomes prayer. Benedictines gather in communities and carry out their lives in that community. During the Middle Ages their monasteries were numerous. Everyone gathered seven times a day for prayer, and everyone had a job. Some tended sheep, others cared for gardens, some took care of the sick, others cooked, some cut wood, some mucked out stables, others cleaned, some cared for the sacred vessels used in worship, some sang, some led, others greeted people at the door, some distributed food and clothing to the poor, some studied, some copied manuscripts, others preached and celebrated Eucharist. You get the picture. What was remarkable is that they saw all of this as prayer, as what they offered to God. And their work/prayer changed the face of the western world. Hospitals and universities arose from monasteries, knowledge of caring for crops and animals increased, books were written and libraries set up to contain and categorize them, they were the original nursing homes and orphanages, and the list goes one. They were both lay and ordained. But they all sensed their call to offer themselves in service to Christ.

How about you?

DISCUSSION QUESTIONS

First, attempt your own brief definition of ordination.

Second, do you think baptism can be seen as ordination to all forms of ministry? If so, how does that work?

Three, talk with a priest and find out what she or he does during a typical week.

Four, to what ministries might Christ be calling you, based on your skills, interest, and experiences?

Chapter 23

Resurrection
The Victory of God

IF YOU WERE TO say to me, "Explain the resurrection," I would have to reply, "I can't." It came about as an utterly unique event with no parallels in human experience. That's part of the reason I can't explain it. I can make no analogies otherwise, nor can I extrapolate from other events. Moreover, I know of no explanation, scientific or otherwise, that offers a description or clarification of what happened on that first Easter. It remains firmly in the category of mystery.

But I can narrate the events of Jesus' last days and the story of what happened on the other side of his burial.

- Jesus was betrayed by one of his own disciples, tried in a kangaroo court, humiliated and abused by soldiers, made to carry his own cross, and crucified in one of the most horrible means of death ever devised.

- He was deserted by his disciples and friends even as he was subjected to humiliation and rejection. His death marked the apparent failure of his life's work.

- He was buried in a small cave according to the burial customs of the Jewish people at that time.

- With the rolling of a huge stone across the entrance to the burial cave we arrive at the tragic end to the story of a heroic man.

- But then occurs the most stupendous surprise in human history.

- Some women followers go to Jesus' tomb on Sunday, and find that it is empty, containing only his burial clothes. When they reported this to the apostles, the women's report seemed to be an "idle tail" and they did not believe them. (Lk 24: 11)
- Then the Risen Christ appears to a number of people. St. Paul gives an inventory of these witnesses. (1 Cor. 15: 3–8)
- The disciples who had once deserted Jesus became bold witnesses to his ministry, death, and resurrection. (Acts 2)

Please note that I have used narration to talk about resurrection. The New Testament itself does not describe the event of resurrection itself, but only the two crucial factors, the empty tomb and the resurrection appearances. And as I have said, it does not attempt to explain the event. What the New Testament does is simply tell the story. And we continue that narrative task today. For example, in the eucharistic prayers of The Episcopal Church some form of the Memorial Acclamation takes place: Christ has died, Christ is risen. Christ will come again. This, of course, states the good news of the gospel in three short declarations.

Allow me now to offer five statements of what we can state by way understanding the resurrection of Christ. First, the New Testament describes a resurrection, not resuscitation or a paranormal experience. Resurrection declares that Jesus died, was buried, and on the third day was raised from the dead by the power of God, and now lives beyond the dominion of death.

Two, the resurrection represents an act of God by which God vindicated Jesus' ministry and death. It was God's seal of approval on Jesus' life and ushered in the kingdom of God.

Three, witnesses carried far and abroad the news of resurrection. It was a word-of-mouth affair. Imagine what you might do if someone you trusted reported to you the resurrection. Would you trust the report? Would you say your friend was deluded or maybe even crazy? What if your friend talked with you at length about seeing, touching, hearing, and even eating with the Risen One? Would that make a difference? What the scripture record does show is that the witnesses, now bold and energized, had once been the very people who deserted Jesus out of fear for their own lives. That remarkable change, I think, can only be explained by a resurrection.

Four, the resurrection was God's victory of sin and death. I am convinced that the power enabling resurrection is the love and life of God. Not even death, universally the most powerful force in the universe, can conquer the God made manifest in Christ. And we can extend this by defining sin as whatever separates us from God. If God can conquer death, then, in the final analysis, sin can be conquered as well.

Five, the Risen Christ continues to be active in the lives of his people, the church. The promised and dependable ways are word and sacrament. In the proclaiming, preaching, and teaching of the scripture as centered in and interpreted by Christ, the Risen Lord makes himself present. In effect, he speaks to us. Have you every had a biblical passage leap from the page and speak a word you needed to hear? Has a sermon ever changed your heart or mind? Also, the sacraments, especially Baptism and Eucharist, are means of Christ's presence. They are acts that dramatize God's grace. Think of them as kisses from God.

Finally, we must highlight the paschal mystery. The ancient word of Easter was "pascha," and that is the root of the term. The Easter story consists of two parts: dying and rising. Through our baptism into the death and resurrection of Christ we share in the paschal mystery. When God is present and active in our lives and in the life of the church the pattern will be according to the paschal mystery. It will be movement from dying to rising, the fear to hope, from evil to holiness, from death to life. Christ's resurrection served not just him, but us, too. We share in resurrection life! If there is better news than that, I do not know it.

DISCUSSION QUESTIONS

First, what is the difference between resuscitation and resurrection?

Second, in 1 Cor 15: 35–49 Paul tries to explain the resurrection body of Jesus. Read this passage and summarize it. He continues in verses 50–57 to tell us of its implication for us. Read this, too, and describe your reaction.

Three, what would your reaction be if you were in Jerusalem in about 30 AD and one of the apostles told you of his experiences with the Risen Lord?

Four, can you think of instances of the paschal mystery in your life and that of your church?

Chapter 24

Revelation
Unveiling the Unknown

SOME YEARS BACK MY daughter wrangled passes for us to visit the Magic Castle in Hollywood. It is a private club for magicians, but with the right connections you can get in. There are magic shows in several large rooms and lots of acts in various corners and alcoves of the old mansion. We found ourselves watching a magician, who was sitting a table performing card and coin tricks. He asked me to help him, and I agreed. He put a quarter in my right hand, told me to hold it tightly, and to extend my hand so that all could see it. He waved his hand in my direction, and I could feel the quarter disappear from my clutch, and it reappeared in the palm of the magician. I have no explanation for this; all I can say is that I clearly sensed the coin leave my grasp. My question then and now is: how did he do that?

What I wanted to know was a matter of revelation. I desired to understand the trick, to have him reveal the secret of his magic. But I know that magicians never reveal their tricks.

Revelation is one of the ways we know, one of the means by which learn and understand.

There are at least four ways we know. For example, we know that the earth is round, and most of us learned that because a teacher told us. This constitutes knowledge by authority. We accept the word of someone we trust and whom we believe to be telling the truth.

Sometimes we know by experience. When I was learning to swim my mother assured me I would float, but I did not entirely trust her on that. I had to jump into the pool, and with the help of an instructor experienced the fact that I do float. It happened to me, and I knew it to be true on the basis of that experience.

Reasoning is another mode of knowing. The little town I grew up in had many silver maple trees; they were on every street. A friend told me that when it was going to rain the maple trees turned over their leaves so that the silver side faced up. So, when I saw dark clouds rolling in, noticed the wind increasing, and observed the silver side of the maple leaves, I could put those facts together and come to a reasonable conclusion: rain was on the way.

And that brings us to revelation, perhaps the most elusive of the ways we know. A revelation is when someone makes known to us something that we could not have known by the other ways of knowing. It consists of pulling back a veil that had been covering something. It is a flashlight in a dark room, or even a magician telling you his secret.

Much of our knowledge about God depends on God's self-revelation. St. Paul in Romans presents us with an important instance. He notes in 1: 19–20 that God has revealed some of the divine nature when we look at the world around us. We will sense God's eternal power and divine nature revealed through what God has created. Thus, he writes, "For what can be known about God is plain to them. Ever since the creation of the world his eternal power and divine nature, invisible though they are, have been understood and seen through the things he made." This has often been titled natural revelation.

But in most of the Bible God' revelation takes place in and through God's actions in history. Certainly the story of the Exodus stands as a prime instance. The story is told in Exodus 13–15. The people of God found themselves in slavery in Egypt. God called Moses to confront Egypt's pharaoh and demand the release of the Israelites. The ruler refused the demands, and God through the agency of Moses inflicted on the Egyptians ten, increasingly painful plagues, the last being the death of all the first-born sons of the country. Pharaoh relents and releases the slaves, who flee east into the desert, hoping to return to their home in Israel. In the meantime, Pharaoh changes his mind and dispatches his army to bring the people back. Soon the slaves are faced with a crisis: in front of them is the Red Sea and in back is the Egyptian army. They are trapped. At this horrible impasse God acts and raises a wind to blow apart the water of the sea so as to allow the

Israelites to pass to the other side. When the army attempts to follow, the wind ceases and the army is drowned.

I suppose that if an outside observer had watched these events, he or she might conclude that the slaves were mighty lucky. But the Israelites believed that the God of their ancestors had made a covenant, a compact, with them to bless and protect them. They, therefore, saw in these events the hand of their God. And they sensed that God had revealed some crucial insights into God's nature. They sensed that their God was faithful to the covenant, that God loved freedom and set people free, that God hears prayer, and that God chooses to bless God's people. Little wonder that the story of the Exodus is often considered the most important and defining event in the Hebrew scriptures. Christians affirm that the consummation of God's revelation occurs in Jesus Christ. The great hymn to the supremacy of Christ in Colossians sums up the revelation.

> He is the image of the invisible God, the firstborn of all creation; for in him all things in heaven and earth were created, things visible and invisible . . . all things have been created through him and for him. He himself is before all things, and in him all things hold together. He is the head of the body, the church; he is the beginning, the firstborn from the dead, so that he might come to have first place in everything. For in him all the fullness of God was pleased to dwell, and through him God was pleased to reconcile to himself all things, whether on earth or in heaven, by making peace through the blood of the cross (Col 1: 15–20)

Furthermore, Christians read all the biblical revelation through Jesus, especially through his death and resurrection. We affirm him both as the measure of and the interpretive principle regarding the revelation of God. Consider, for example, the Red Sea story, an event that occurred some fifteen hundred years before Christ, and yet we can see what that event revealed about God coincides with what Jesus revealed about God. In the liturgical tradition of the church, the Exodus story takes a prominent part in the Great Vigil of Easter, and in that setting is seen as a type or analogue of the journey from death to life through the waters of baptism, a journey characteristic of all Christians.

The Christ revelation also works the other way. In eighteenth century Europe a philosophy called Deism became popular. Among its tenets was the idea that God created the world and the laws of nature, and then withdrew. They compared it to the workings of a clock; God created it and wound it, and then stepped aside. The biblical revelation, especially as focused in Jesus, replies a definitive No. Jesus reveals God as intimately involved with the world and its people, and that involvement is characterized by compassion and blessing.

The ancient prophet Jeremiah looked for a day when God would make a new covenant, a new way of relating to God's people. The prophet proclaimed that God would write the divine law on the hearts of people, that they all would know themselves to be God's people, and that God would forgive and forget their sins. The Christian witness is that this old prophecy found its fulfillment in Christ, especially in terms of the gift of the Holy Spirit to the church at Pentecost.

I must note here that biblical revelation is not usually obvious. That is, divine revelation does not make itself so stunningly clear that there is no other explanation of it source other than from God. Christians say that Jesus is Lord; indeed, this may have been the earliest Christian creed. But others might read the gospels and come to other conclusions, such as Jesus was a good man and a great teacher of wisdom but not the revelation of God. We are speaking here of the mystery of faith. Some seem to have it and some do not. I certainly cannot give a quick and clean answer to this issue. All I can do is testify to my experience and pray that that might serve as a moment of revelation for others.

I must add that the last book of the Bible is entitled "Revelation," or more properly "The Revelation of St. John the Divine." The writer states that, in fact, the book is a revelation of Jesus Christ, given to him through an angel. (Rev 1: 1) He goes on to report that this testimony of Jesus came to him on a Sunday and was spoken by a loud voice like a trumpet. (1: 9–10) The book of Revelation comes to us in the form of an apocalypse, and, thus, uses the convention of revealing the future of the people of God. In fact, the book's revelation is a spinning out of the death and resurrection of Jesus: God is faithful to God's people, God will bless God's people, and that God will be victorious in the great struggle against evil.

Sometimes revelation comes in small and ordinary ways. I had the honor of being the master of a wonderful springer spaniel named Lizzie. For sixteen years she was my nearly constant companion. When I first acquired her several people told me that "dog" is God spelled backward. That seemed perfectly obvious and rather corny to me. As time passed I began to sense that she was something of a revelation of God. She was always eager to see me, never content unless she was with me, and clearly cared about me. I began to find myself saying, "If this beautiful little dog can be that faithful, what must God be like?" She helped reveal to me the depth of God's love, and I loved her for it.

DISCUSSION QUESTIONS:

First, can you identify some breakthrough, revelatory moments in your relationship with God?

Second, what about God was revealed to you in those moments?

Three, I have noted that divine revelation is usually open to other interpretations and explanations. What role does faith play in sensing a revelatory event?

Four, some people say that they discover God in nature. Do you have any experience with this? If so, what was revealed to you?

Chapter 25

Sacraments
Visible and Invisible

One summer my family and I were on a vacation trip, and when Sunday rolled around we decided to visit a church. We participated in a well-done liturgy with fine preaching in a beautiful building. We went to the altar rail to receive Communion. I was holding the hand of our older daughter and my wife held our younger daughter, who was about two years old. That particular congregation did not commune young and unconfirmed children. As we walked back to our pew, our younger one started to scream at the top of her considerably loud voice, "I want my bread! I want my bread!" Rachel sensed two things. First, something important was going on. And second, she had been left out.

The church does, indeed, consider the sacraments to be very important. They, in fact, stand at the heart of the life of the church and define who and what a Christian is. That is, we can define a Christian as a baptized person who communes. For example, think of how most of the churches you have visited are arranged. Most would contain a minimum of four things: an altar for Eucharist, a font for baptism, a pulpit or ambo for the reading and preaching of the Word, and chairs on which participants sit. Even the architecture proclaims the centrality of the sacraments.

The two great sacraments, baptism and Eucharist, come to us at the command of Jesus: "Go therefore and make disciples of all nation, baptizing them in the name of the Father and of the Son and of the Holy Spirit," (Matt 28: 19) and "'This is my body that is for you. Do this in remembrance of me . . . This cup is the new covenant in my blood. Do this, as often as you drink it, in remembrance of me.'" (1 Cor 11: 24–25) Because they come from the Lord himself we refer to them as the dominical sacraments, and Christians see them as essential for salvation.

A usual definition for sacraments states that they are outward and visible signs of the invisible, inward grace given by Christ himself as means by which we are both given and receive that grace. I myself like to think of them as little dramas, significant events which make use of common elements such as water, wine, and bread by which the Risen One mediates his presence and favor to us. Consider this analogy. I could say to you, "I love you." Or, I could give you a kiss, which is an action that conveys the same message as the spoken statement. Think of the sacraments as Christ's kisses for his people.

So far I have written about the two great sacraments. But many churches, including my own Episcopal Church, would say that there are five more sacraments. Over the centuries Christians have played a lengthy game of push-and-shove about the number of sacraments. In one sense, any actions that conveys Christ's presence could be called a sacrament, could it not? A hot meal for a hungry person in the church undercroft might qualify. A heartfelt hug for a lonely person might mediate the Lord's merciful presence. But in the twelfth century Peter Lombard enumerated seven sacraments and that has come to be accepted by many, but not all, churches.

In this view we have two great sacraments commanded by Christ and understood to be necessary for salvation. Along with these are five others that developed in the life of the church as directed by the Holy Spirit. They are: confirmation, ordination, marriage, reconciliation, and anointing with oil and laying on of hands for healing.

Let's take a brief look at these lesser sacraments, sometimes called sacramental acts. Confirmation involves a person reaffirming baptismal vows and receiving the laying on of hands by the bishop for the strengthening of that person in her or his baptismal living. Ordination again involves the laying on of episcopal hands with prayer to set apart and empower a person to be a deacon, priest, or bishop. Marriage consists of vows of lifelong and exclusive faithfulness between two persons along with a blessing for the strengthening of their live together. Reconciliation denotes a person confessing sins to a priest and receiving an absolution, that is, an announcement that his or her sins have been forgiven. Finally, we have the anointing with holy oil, called unction, with the laying on the hands for the healing of mind, body, and spirit.

In fairness I need to point out that certain Protestant churches do not practice sacraments in the sense we have been using that term. They say that baptism is a witness act, a way of stating that a person is committed to Christ. Further, the Eucharist, which they usually prefer to call the Lord's Supper, is an act to help Christians remember that Christ died for them. In neither case is there a sense that Christ is present mediating his graceful presence to participants. Usually they refer to these two events as ordinances and are reluctant to use the term sacrament. I would venture to say that they view preaching in sacramental event, although they would not say that explicitly.

But catholic Christians always understand the two great sacraments as radical and transformational events. They represent the good news of Jesus in action. Think of what happens to a baptismal candidate. That person is united to Christ's death and resurrection, and is given the gift of the Holy Spirit. Sins are forgiven and the person becomes part of the Body of Christ, the church. In baptism Christ makes an unbreakable and eternal covenant with the candidate, promising to know and love that person always and in all circumstances. When you put all of this together, I believe we need to think of baptism as a miraculous event, a time-and-space events in which Christ himself enters a person's life and changes that person's identity.

Holy Eucharist is no less dramatic. In the giving and receiving of bread and wine Christ makes himself present, and the communicant actually takes Christ into his or her body. Christ lives in them, and they live in Christ. To express how real and concrete this exchange is the church speaks of the Body and Blood of Christ and of the fact that he is actually present. Thus, this sacrament represents the renewal of our relationship with Jesus, forgiveness and a new beginning, strength for the journey through life. We can say that we dine with Jesus, who is both the host and the meal. This becomes, then, the Sunday meal for the baptized family of God.

For a short time a graham cracker company used as its slogan "You've eaten the best news of the week." Does that not better describe Eucharist better than it does crackers?

Sacramental churches face some issues. That is what we need to explore next. First, ordained priests and bishops are curators of the sacraments. Their training forms them in the spirituality and practice of sacramental living, and their ordination both authorizes and empowers their role as celebrants and presiders of the sacraments. They are to teach congregants about the meaning of the sacraments and how to live into them, and they are to protect the sacramental life of the church from distortions. As you may sense, the sacraments are central to the life of priests.

And it works the other way, as well. Because the sacraments are so central to the life of the Christian community—they both "make" or establish the church as well as sustain the life of the church—the sacraments need special handling; therefore, presiding at the sacraments falls only to priests and bishops.

Second, the topic of the baptism of infants can always generate a lively discussion. To start we need to say that adult baptism stands as the norm for baptismal practice. That's because it joins faith with the sacramental action. A person with commitment to Christ receives the graces of baptism and promises to live a life shaped by that fact. But even in the New Testament we find another practice. Some texts note that whole households were baptized, and that presumably included children. Acts 17: 33 stands as an example. Paul and Silas had been imprisoned, but a providential earthquake rattled open the doors. The jailer was in despair about losing prisoners. But Paul takes the occasion to evangelize the jailer, who was with his whole family baptized. The assumption in such cases was that the little one would be reared in such a way that he or she would come to commitment later in life. Eventually western culture reached a point where it was thoroughly Christianized so that nearly all people were baptized as infants. The commitment came later at the rite of confirmation, when the person made a public statement of faith using the ancient baptismal Apostles' Creed. So, then, the traditional practice included the baptism of infants and children. As stated, that must be accompanied by the good possibility that the child will reach a place of faith.

I myself was baptized when I was about two months old, and therefore have no memory of it. I have, however, come to value that fact. For me it places the emphasis on the action and the initiative of God. I am encouraged by the idea that God chose me and accepted me before I could respond; God took a chance on me. The grandeur of grace comes to the fore clearly and forcefully.

Next, how much water should we use when baptizing? This, too, has been a subject of controversy in some places. The ancient tradition was to use "living water," which suggests a stream or a spring. Furthermore, the basic imagery of baptism as a dying and rising in Christs does not work unless people can watch a person actually being put under water. Nevertheless, over the centuries fonts became smaller and the use of living water ceased. I certainly have seen baptismal fonts in which the water container was no bigger than a cereal bowl. Current practice is to move back to baptismal pools when churches are being built or renovated, and to use as much water as possible even with small fonts. I trust that God can use whatever amount of water we use in order to mediate saving grace.

Finally, we come to a more complicated problem, namely, the communing of unbaptized persons. The invitation to the partake is offered to anyone, baptized or not. I have, indeed, heard an invitation to commune even if you were part of another religion. This practice started fairly recently and is confined, as far as I can tell, to this country. People who advocate this practice do so in the name a radical hospitality, celebrating the fact that God accepts all people. However, in light of what we have said about both baptism and Eucharist, this open invitation seems anomalous if not absurd. The Eucharist is an encounter with the living Lord, and to my mind requires some careful thought and preparation. Furthermore, the scripture seems to warn against it. Matt 22: 11 ff. is the story of the man cast out of the marriage banquet because he is not wearing a wedding robe. The traditional interpretation states that the wedding robe is the righteousness given by God at baptism. In 1 Cor 11: 19–32 Paul addresses an issue in the Corinthian congregation. Some get drunk and others do not show honor to other members. He says that they must examine themselves, remembering that it is the Lord's supper that they eat. Communing the unbaptized cannot be supported on either theological or biblical grounds.

I hope you have come to sense what an awesome event it is to participate in the sacraments. To emphasize that more, let me note that the sacraments are based on the fact of the incarnation, the God took on flesh and dwelled among us. If God can take on the materiality of flesh and blood, then it surely follows that God can make God's self available and present in water, bread, and wine. If Christmas can happen, then baptism and Eucharist can happen.

Finally, we could not consider the sacraments without noting that they call for us to live sacramentally, both to live into and live out of the facts that we are baptized and are in communion with Christ. It helps, I believe, to think of the sacraments as miracles. In baptism, God has ripped open the sky, grabbed us, and told us that we will always belong to him no matter what. And I am the object of that divine action; that stuns me. At the Eucharist I am given the living Christ, and share in his resurrection life together with baptized around the world and with all those saints who have gone before. Again, I am the object of that divine action, and it stuns me. The sacraments help me see myself as God sees me, and that changes my sense of who I am, my identity. Moreover, they ask me to live as if I really am in communion with Christ.

The Episcopal Church's Book of Common Prayer contains a remarkable instance. Part of the liturgy for baptism is called "The Baptismal Covenant." It takes the form of questions and answers. Three regard belief and use the ancient "baptismal symbol," that is, the Apostles' Creed. Do you believe in God the Father, God the Son, and God the Holy Spirit? Then follow five questions about living our baptism:

1. Will you continue in the apostle's teaching and fellowship, in the breaking of bread, and in the prayers? Reply: I will, with God's help.

2. Will you persevere in resisting evil, and, whenever you fall into sin, repent and return to the Lord? Reply: I will, with God's help.

3. Will you proclaim by word and example the Good News of God in Christ? Reply: I will, with God's help.

4. Will you seek and serve Christ in all persons, loving your neighbor as yourself? Reply: I will, with God's help.

5. Will you strive for justice and peace among all people, and respect the dignity of every human being? Reply: I will, with God's help. (Book of Common Prayer, pp. 304–305)

The God who encounters us in scripture is always holy and seeks people to be holy. That means we live with a constant call to display a lifestyle that recognizes that we belong to God in Christ, that we are valued without limit, and that God carries on God's mission through us. We follow Christ with gladness and singleness of heart. We love him, because he first loved us. And that makes all the difference!

DISCUSSION QUESTIONS

First, do you know when and where you were baptized?

Second, how do you prepare yourself to receive communion?

Three, if you were to use the Baptismal Covenant noted above, how are you doing?

Four, which do you think is more appropriate to receiving communion, sorrow over sin or celebration of Christ's forgiving presence? Why?

Chapter 26

Sacrifice
What We Offer to God

Suppose we took a trip across time and space to a city in the ancient world, perhaps Corinth or Ephesus. One of the elements of the cityscape that likely would strike us would the large number of temples. Each would be dedicated to one of the multitude of gods that inhabited the imaginations of the people. They often presented a spectacular appearance, and many would have smoke rising from their precincts. Sacrifice was being made, often incense, bread, perfume, but most of all animals. With the last item, the beast was killed and the flesh or blood or both were offered to the god. So, we should expect to see and smell lots of blood.

In these ancient cities the temples themselves were a type of sacrifice, devotees having given over the building to one of the gods. As we look at both the building and what happens there we cannot but sense that some sort of important transaction is taking place. And, in fact, the people believed the temple to be the proper place to encounter the divine and to give to the particular god a gift. In the most ancient settings, the idea was to feed the god, and thereby insure the god's happiness. Or the offering was made to appease for a wrong. But beneath all these motives stood the need to insure the favor of the god. For example, someone might offer a sheep to ask for a good crop of wheat or a generous rainfall during the planting season. The offering of sacrifice was, then, a deadly serious matter.

We today tend to understand religion as inward and private, but for ancient cultures it was outward and public. Our culture likes to file religion under the category of those who might be inclined to pursue divine affairs, but for ancients it was a life-and-death concern. We like to think that religious matters should be inexpensive, if not free; think of the people who offer to God a dollar in the offering plate. The ancient people believed that their lives depended on keeping the gods happy, and they sacrificed the best they had. I think the parallel would be to say that when they offered a bull we today would have to hand over one of our cars. The gods and sacrifice were knotted together; we today have untied the knot.

Several years back I was in Taipei for a meeting. As we drove through the streets of that busy and modern city I was fascinated by the various temples that stood on street corners. Fortress-like and ornately carved, they were painted in bright colors so that they could not be ignored. I learned that inside these structures a number of activities occurred. People sought out fortune tellers or healers. Some tried to honor or commune with dead relatives. All of these, of course, involved the sacrifice of money or the purchase of incense or candles. The temples were dedicated to no one religion, but clearly were places where people played out the deep workings of their hearts. I had to respect it, even though I do not think I fully comprehended it. Note, however, that at root they were places where people offered something, sacrificed something, to be touched by the mystery of the divine.

We have taken some time to try to imagine our way in the importance of sacrifice for people in the past and for some today. They understand it as essential to the way human beings related to the gods; they knew it as an integral part of their transactions with their gods.

As you might expect, however, what the Bible has to say about sacrifice both parallels and diverges from the practice of non-scriptural cultures. Let's take a brief look at the worship of the Israelites of the Hebrew Bible. They had four annual festivals involving sacrifice. They were:

1. Passover. This probably began as a celebration of lambing season, but later recalled the Exodus from Egypt by the Israelites. Lambs were sacrificed

2. Pentecost, also called Weeks. This marked the end of the wheat harvest, but also remembered the giving of God's law at Mt. Sinai.

3. Tabernacles, also called Booths. This coincided with the end of the growing season, and celebrated the wilderness wandering of the Israelites in the desert after their exodus from Egypt.

The fourth, Atonement, was perhaps the most important. The rites involved purifying the people, the priests, and the Temple itself. Bulls, goats, and incense were given to God as sacrifices. As a side note, incense was imported from the southern arabian peninsula; it consisted of the resin of the frankincense shrub, and was an expensive imported product. The heart of the celebration focused on a goat, which was known as the scape goat. The high priest confessed the sins of the people while laying his hands on the head of the goat, which was then driven out into the wilderness. Aspects of this ceremony elude scholars, but clearly the goat is offered as a sacrifice which bears the sins of the nation.

The Temple in Jerusalem stood at the very center of these proceedings. Built by Solomon it was one of the wonders of the world, but for the Israelites it marked the place where God dwelled in a special, unique way. The various ceremonies were presided over by the divinely instituted priesthood; this was an inherited office, all priests being descendants of Aaron.

The purpose of the sacrifices, festivals, and of the existence of the Temple itself was to acknowledge the Lord as God, to deal with guilt, to atone for unintentional sins, and to make up for ritual impurity (for example, touching a dead body rendered you impure in God's sight). In general, all this was to set things right with God, the one who created and sustained all things and who was the savior and protector of the people of Israel. There was, however, a catch: the sacrificial system with its attendant priesthood could not compensate for heavy and intentional sins. By the eighth century BC the prophets launched a critique of the sacrificial system, the Temple, and the priesthood. Here is a classic example from Amos. God speaks.

> I hate, I despise your festivals, and I take no delight in your solemn assemblies. Even though you offer me your burnt offerings and grain offerings, I will not accept them; and the offerings of well-being of your fatted animals I will not look upon. Take away from me the noise of your songs; I will not listen to the melody of your harps. But let justice roll down like waters, and righteousness like an everflowing stream. Amos 5: 21–24

In general these prophets advocated an integrity of will, mind, and heart. They pointed out that ritual could overlook the issue of exclusive loyalty of God and compassion for the poor. Their divine message stated that God wanted righteous living and justice for all people.

SACRIFICE

When we turn to the New Testament we are greeted with a radical reinterpretation of sacrifice. When Jesus first appears in the fourth gospel John the Baptist points to him and exclaims, "Look, here is the Lamb of God." (John 1: 36) Jesus has now become the sacrificial victim that played such an important role in the Temple system.

Again in the fourth gospel Jesus soon after the above event upsets the while sacrificial system. You can read the episode in John 2: 13–23. Early in his public ministry Jesus travels to Jerusalem and, as you would expect, immediately goes to the Temple. The courts around the Temple are swarming with animals, and money changers are busy at work. Since Roman coins had imprinted on them images of the emperor they were considered unclean by Jewish people. In order to purchase animals for the prescribed sacrifices the people exchanged their currency for Temple coins, which had no images on them. Of course, a fee was involved and the Temple personnel profited. Jesus makes a whip of cords, drives out the animals, and overturns the tables of the money changers. I hope you sense that this action echoes the prophecy of Amos quoted above. This marks Jesus' radical critique of the sacrificial system.

But he goes further. The Temple authorities rightly ask about his right to do this. They want a sign, some mandate, from God for his action. He replied, "'Destroy this temple, and in three days I will raise it up.'" (John 2: 19) He was speaking metaphorically of himself, and pointing to what will be the great sign, the divine mandate, namely, his resurrection. His astonishing claim is that he is now the Temple, the special dwelling place of God. Not only that, but, as the previous comment by the Baptist shows, he is also the sacrifice. It does not take much imagination to see that this is eventually going to lead to disaster.

We are now about to dive into deep water. At this point I hope you sense that in our discussion of sacrifice we are analyzing a central concept of religion in general and of the Bible specifically. Sacrifice seems to be need almost hard-wired into human beings. We have lived among mysterious powers, divine powers, powers beyond our control and we must offer sacrifice. To review we have looked at sacrifice in ancient religion, in the Old Testament, and at Jesus as both the lamb of God and as the new Temple. But more remains to be said.

The book of Hebrews in the New Testament contains an extensive discussion of sacrifice in chapters nine and ten. Allow me to summarize some of the salient points of the writer's analysis.

The prophetic critique of the sacrificial system has been taken seriously, and the writer simply states that the offering of bulls and other items does not deal with sin. He emphatically states that animal sacrifice cannot erase sin. In other words, human action cannot alter the fact of sin, the fact that a great gulf separates God and humanity. He assumes that his readers will take this situation seriously and recognize it as a tragedy. Today many may need a reminder that the basic issues that ail us are rooted in this alienation from God: guilt, fear, a sense of purposeless, loneliness, cruelty, violence, poverty, and anxiety. The writer suggests that the sacrificial system is, at best, a pleading for divine favor and a sign that God choses to step across the gulf and grant favor.

In chapters nine and ten the main message declares the Jesus is the perfect high priest who offers the perfect sacrifice of his own sinless self via the cross and this act is a once and for all matter. Christ alone sets things right with God, so that we can approach God with confidence in God's mercy and favor. As you see this thoroughly reinterprets the traditional sacrificial system. One might be tempted to read this as a mythological statement, but, in fact, it is myth that took place in time and space. God was acting in and through Jesus in the most concrete way to take the initiative, bridge the gulf of sin, and envelope sinful humanity in divine compassion.

So, we have entered a new reality where the gospel turns traditional religion inside-out. Instead of humanity offering sacrifices to God in order to appease or atone, God offers God's self to humanity in the person of Jesus Christ. And in Christ, God does not stint, but rather offers the fulness of who God is in an act of total commitment and faithfulness to humanity. Let's be clear: it is God who sacrifices God's own self.

This opens a door to a new reality of the radical availability of grace. I want to emphasize just here that we do not and, in truth, should not explain the cross or the perfect high priesthood of Jesus in terms of penal substitutionary metaphors; we should not think of Jesus as God's whipping boy or of God demanding the death of his own son as a way to deal with sin. While this approach may have had some interpretive power to medieval people it today comes close to suggesting to us today that God must be cruel and compassionless. No! God was acting in Christ, not Christ acting on God. To put it simply and positively, God has taken the lead in setting things right.

With that we end our look at Hebrews. While rather complicated I hope it helps reveal the richness of the Christian concept of sacrifice.

SACRIFICE

But how are we to respond? What are implications for the way we conduct our lives? First, respond we should. And gratitude and thanksgiving are good places to start. But this does not come easily for most of us. We must be taught it. For instance, I recently gave a disposable fountain pen to the son of a staff member. His mother paused for a second, and then prompted from him the proper response, "What do you say." As someone has said, thanksgiving is just good manners to God. And with that, gratitude can grow into full-blown praise to God.

But there's more. This compassion, this mercy, this love of God serves as a battering ram against our persistent self-interest and concentration on ourselves. This turning in on ourselves exists as the basic element of sin and serves as the means of blocking God out of our lives. But this love of God revealed in Jesus' incarnation, death, and resurrection can leap over the walls of selfishness and begin the process of forming Christ in us, the process that can lead to lives of praise to Christ and service to others.

Once we get this fixed in our minds we can return to the sacrifice that we might offer to God. The apostle Paul sums it up for us. "I appeal to you therefore, brothers and sister, by the mercies of God, to present your bodies as a living sacrifice, holy and acceptable to God, which is your spiritual worship. Do not be conformed to this word, but be transformed by the renewing of your minds, so that you may discern what is the will of God." (Rom 12: 1–2) In the preceeding eleven chapters Paul has stated his particular way of understanding the gospel, and then he comes to the great "therefore." Our response to the God's sacrifice is to offer back to God the sacrifice of our whole selves. He assures us that God will accept that sacrifice as a proper act of worship. Part of that sacrifice is the renewing of our minds, that is, offering our minds, so that we are able to discern God's will. This does not require bulls and sheep but rather the offering of our selves. For Christian people our sacrifice is always a thankful response to God's steadfast mercy.

Throughout my life I have had many roles to play. In college I was a student, and during the summers a factory worker. Later I was a priest and more recently a bishop. But I have also had the honor of being a husband, a father, a son, a sibling. All of us have various roles in life. But what if we were to sense these as vocations, as calls from God, as opportunities to perceive the gracious action of God in our lives and to offer the sacrifice of praise and thanksgiving to God? Would that not transform the way we live? Would we not gladly be living sacrifices to God?

THE LANGUAGE OF LOVE
DISCUSSION QUESTIONS

First, how do you react to the idea that God offered the ultimate sacrifice to us in Jesus?

Second, are there occasions in your life where you have made significant sacrifices? If so, what are they?

Third, what are the emotional and inner dynamics involved in the sacrifice of praise to God? What are your sacrificing?

Fourth, in what ways can whole congregations become communities of sacrifice?

Chapter 27

Salvation

To Be Safe and Sound

EVERYONE LOVES THE STORY of Jonah. He had been called by God to proclaim a message of salvation to Nineveh, the capital city of Israel's greatest enemy. Jonah adamantly did not want to be involved in giving that city an opportunity to repent, so he got on a ship sailing in exactly the opposite direction. A great storm arises, and the sailor sense that someone's god is punishing a person aboard the ship. "Oh, I'm the one," declares Jonah. And the sailors toss him overboard. As he sinks into the sea, a great fish swallows him, and he remains in the belly of the animal for three days. Finally Jonah gets down to the business of prayer, and he ends his prayer with the phrase "Deliverance belongs to the LORD!". (2: 9) And at that the fish spews up Jonah on dry land.

Of course, Jonah's declaration stands as the major point of this tale and of the whole Bible. In both the languages of scripture, Hebrew and Greek, the word "salvation" means deliverance, to be placed in a place of being safe and sound, and being liberated from danger and oppression.

The Old Testament always understands God as the preeminent savior and deliverer; salvation belongs to God. Now, I need to say that sometimes men and women are called saviors. Think of Deborah or David. But they are regarded as agent of God's salvation. God works through human agents with the constant intent to saving, delivering, and liberating the people of Israel.

This perception changed, however, in the period between Malachi, the last of the prophets, and John the Baptist (about 300 BC till 25 AD). No prophets appeared in Israel, and, therefore, the people had no word of God to guide them. Moreover, they suffered terribly at the hands of the Seleucid rulers. They began to view the world as so evil that nothing less than a direct intervention by God could save them. We can identify this as the apocalyptic mindset, a sense that the world is engulfed in darkness and evil so profound that God will have to call a halt to the whole thing. You may sense that many today have developed this attitude, wondering if the human story can continue on its present course. For example, how many movies have you seen recently where humanity is portrayed in danger of extinction from everything from climate change to space aliens.

But returning to scripture, then Jesus appears. He proclaims the advent of the Kingdom of God and models what it looks like. The Kingdom appears as acts of salvation in and through Jesus. The gospels narrate the exorcisms of Jesus. He is able to cast out the forces of evil that ruin the lives of people. He liberates people from disease and even from death. Indeed, he frees people from their apocalyptic mindset by announcing that they are delivered from the wrath to come.

The epistles of the New Testament take a more existential approach. Consider the following:

- The work of Christ moves the world from darkness to light (the whole of the gospel of John and also 1 Pet 2: 9),
- From alienation to citizenship in God's kingdom (1 Pet 2: 10),
- From guilt to pardon (Col 1: 4),
- From slavery to freedom (Gal 5: 1), and
- From fear to liberty (1 John 4: 18).

We have arrived at the place where we can summarize salvation in light of Jesus Christ.

First, salvation addresses the whole person: mind, body, spirit, imagination, and emotion. Modern medical and psychological practice has helped us understand that each of us exists as a unity, that what happens to the body effects the emotions, that an act of the will alters the imagination, and so forth.

Second, salvation results from an act of God and should be understood as a gift of grace. My own experience, for instance, is that we can't heal

SALVATION

ourselves, nor can we understand healing as a process that is either automatic or subject to manipulation. I find salvation, deliverance, and healing have a mysterious element that seems to arrive under its own power. Some years back I engaged in some extensive therapy to deal with issues of emotions and imagination. I had an expert clinical psychologist and found the process very helpful in understanding both my past and some of the ways my mind works. All that, however, only got me so far. To the degree that I am healed, that is, liberated from both parts of my past and my identity, has come as a gift through prayer and spiritual direction. How that happened seems to me to be a gift and a mystery.

Third, the church can be an agent of healing. Think of AA programs, healing services, pastoral care and counseling, and preaching. I find it significant that hospitals had their beginnings in monasteries. These instances stand as programs of the church. But individual Christians living out their baptismal covenant also act as agents of salvation. For example, I am grateful to a grandmother who taught me Bible stories and to college teachers who showed me that Christians need to be involved in such ethical issues as racism and violence.

Fourth, I find that four areas of our lives point us to our need of salvation. We experience these as neuralgic places, thoughts and feelings that keep us awake at night, impulses that make us tick. We all need to deal with guilt and regret. We have all hurt and damaged other people, organizations, and even the earth itself, and we have done this even while sometimes acting out of the best of intentions. We also long for meaning and purpose for our lives. Am I here for a reason? Is there any sense or shape to my life? And how do we face death? Finally, can I be loved? Is it possible that I can be known, accepted, and valued? Unless we can find some peace about these we will not live full lives.

Finally, our focus must be on Jesus. To put it another way, we can interpret our existence through Jesus in such a way that we are caught up in the mystery of salvation. Here I am willing to venture into a controversial place. My experience tells me that it is only in Jesus I can find salvation. When Jesus said "I am the way, and the truth, and the life" (John 14: 6) I can only respond by affirming that as true for me. I willingly admit that others may have other experiences of salvation, but for me it lies with Jesus.

Some years back my wife and I went on a pilgrimage in Scotland. Both she and I have roots in that country and are interested in the holy sites and holy people of that place. Part of our tour took us to the Outer

Hebrides and especially to the Isle of Lewis. We made our way to the far north of that island and stood on the cliffs looking at the wild sea blown by the wind. It felt like the end of the world. We were then taken to a nearby church. The building itself was medieval, but it marked an even more ancient church honoring one St. Moluag. If you look him up you will find that he was a sixth century monk, and not much else. But this little church has a unique aspect to it. The medieval story was that if you spent the night in St. Moluag's Church you would be cured of madness. When our group heard this tidbit, some chuckled, and then we left. But the memory and the feel of that place lingers. It surely seemed a thin place, a holy site, to me. Why is it that we across such places, places that remind us that we all seek salvation in some form? Might this be the Risen One at work? And this place left me with a sense of hope. Salvation might just be possible.

DISCUSSION QUESTIONS

First, where are the place in your life where you need salvation? What about your church?

Second, what aspects of Jesus' life and ministry hold out the hope of salvation most for you?

Three, do you believe you have ever been a means of God's saving work in the lives of others?

Fourth, how can the church better be a medium of Christ's salvation?

Chapter 28

Sin

More Than Missing the Mark

I ADMIT IT. I am an expert on sin. I am not speaking of errors or mistakes or misjudgments. Sin is something more than those factors. I do wish that I simply made errors from which I could extract learning, or that my problems were simply the result of lack of information or mere lapses of judgment. No, I have to confess that it goes deeper than that. I sin.

Here is the heart of sin: me first. Sin represents the slant in our nature in which we want to think of ourselves as the center of the cosmos. The theologians of the Reformation period called it *incurvatus se*, curving in on ourselves, always coming back to ol' number one. If I am honest I have to say that this operates all the time and in all aspects of my life. That's sin. And you and I are experts on it.

In many of the prayers of confession I encounter I run across the admission that we have done things we ought not to have done and have not done things we ought to have done. Fair enough. I can think of dozens of instances of both. I also recognize that I can pass these off as the result of a lack of information or the press of time or simply faulty judgment. And that allows us to say to ourselves, "I may be a sinner, but I'm not a terribly bad one. I've never murdered anyone or robbed a bank."

But those same prayers of confession often continue. They state that we have not loved God with our whole being nor have we loved our neighbor as ourselves. And in saying that we sense we have gone to a deeper level of truth about ourselves. This, I believe, brings us to the heart of the matter.

Sin describes my state of loving myself above all else. It fences out any deep concern for God or for the people in my life. And it causes separation from God and from others. And it represents the source of the pain and anguish of the world. For example, if I have a roof over my head I'm not inclined to worry about the homeless people who hang out in the park next to my office. Or consider this. When you are not thinking about something in particular what do you think about? You think about yourself. And given that we have a difficult time making room for God.

I know that some churches spend too much time and energy talking about sin. And I know that the church can be accused of moralism, that is, of telling people what they have to do to be better, less sinful people. And we can be faulted for sentimentality, simply urging people to be more nice. None of this helps us deal with our sinful nature.

So, then, we turn to the Bible. In the Old Testament we find that sin has seven faces: missing the goal, disharmony, crookedness, rebellion, ritual defilement, guilt, violence, vanity, and just plain wickedness. The people of Israel understood that they lived in a covenant relationship with God. We can say that they believed God had chosen them and married them. This meant that both parties had to live within that covenant. God would have to be faithful, guiding, and protecting of the chosen people. And the Israelites, for their part, would have to be faithful and obedient to God.

The major story of the covenant occurs as the Israelites have escaped from slavery in Egypt and have arrived at the foot of the Mountain of God, sometimes called Mount Sinai and sometimes Mt. Horeb. There God meets the people through their leader Moses. These are the words God commands Moses to deliver to the people:

> You have seen what I did to the Egyptians, and how I bore you on eagles' wings and brought you to myself. Now, therefore, if you obey my voice and keep my covenant, you shall be my treasured possession out of all the peoples. Indeed, the whole earth is mine, but you shall be for me a priestly kingdom and a holy nation. (Exod 19: 4–6)

This covenant was ratified in a solemn ceremony in which the blood of oxen was sprinkled on an altar and on the people. Blood represented life itself to these people. The altar stood in the place of God. They now knew they were linked to God and God to them with blood, with life itself.

I hope you sense that to violate the covenant was to violate God. And that violation would come when they put themselves ahead of God and their connection to him. The result would be injury both the self and to the community.

They came to see God as merciful, but also to see it was hard to live within the covenant, even knowing that it was a relationship of life and love. The prophets arose as spokespersons for God, naming sin and calling people to repentance. The prophets spoke about the need for serious worship, justice, righteous living, care for the poor. This was what it meant to live within a relationship with God.

I above used the analogy of marriage. In general terms it is defined by the vows of lifelong and exclusive love and faithfulness between the two married persons. An episode of adultery would be an obvious violation of the covenant and would certainly cause a major fissure in the marriage. But other, less obvious factors indicate problems. Suppose one member of the couple will not apologize for harsh words, or one member cannot remember to give a compliment. In all these examples we find sin at work, and the result is injury to partners.

When we turn to the New Testament, we note that the synoptic gospels seldom make use of the category of sin. Paul, however, in Rom 1—3 lays out a profound analysis of our topic. He sees sin as a power with almost objective force, and it functions as a sort of spiritual substitute for God. Everything from idolatry to gossip is rooted in this force. And he notes its power in autobiographical terms. "I can will what is right, but I cannot do it. For I do not do the good I want, but the evil I do not want is what I do ... it is no longer I that do it, but sin that dwells within me." (Rom 7: 18–20)

In this section of Romans the point Paul is working toward the conclusion that all people are sinners. Despite that God chooses to be graceful toward us. He says that God is able to justify us, that is, see us as righteous, because of Jesus Christ's death and resurrection. The result is peace between God and God's people.

The locus of God's revelation of divine mercy and compassion is the cross and resurrection. There we watch God jump into the deep end of human suffering and anguish, all caused by sin, and embracing it, carrying it, making it God's own. This represents the ultimate commitment of God to us. And in the resurrection God demonstrates the victory of divine love and life.

John's gospel fits nicely with this. In that gospel, the ultimate sin is not believing in Jesus. The evangelist is saying that we live in separation from

God until we trust that God's true nature is revealed in Jesus and begin to live into that trust. The result, says this gospel, is abundant life.

We have had to wrestle with the subject of sin. If you have read this far I congratulate you on your moxie. Sin describes who we are, but it does not represent a full description. We are also the beloved of God, the people for whom God was willing to invest God's full self. What motivates God is God's desire to save sinners. And that is God's final word on sin.

I once was involved in the Rite of Reconciliation, often called private confession. One lists one's sins to a priest, who offers counsel and absolution. I admit that sitting down in the silence and writing out a list of all the sins you have committed depresses me. And the list, of course, always points to my paltry love of God. On this particular occasion I had worked my way through my list, when I noticed that my confessor was angry with me. He said, "It's always that same list of sins." I was embarrassed and had to admit that he was correct. The next question was: what am I going to do about that. How am I going to live more closely with Jesus?

If there is value in thinking about sin, I believe it lies in those two questions. Yes, I sin, because that's part of who I am, namely, a sinner. But God has taken the stunning step of crossing the gulf between us. So, what is my response? How am I going to orient myself more to Jesus and less toward myself?

What about you?

DISCUSSION QUESTIONS

First, please develop a definition of sin in your own words.

Second, what are signs that God's mercy is greater than our sin?

Three, what might it mean to say that Jesus was sinless?

Four, define repentance.

Chapter 29

Worship
What Is God Worth?

I REMEMBER THE FIRST time I saw a marriage performed according to the Book of Common Prayer in the Church of England. I was struck by what was said as the groom put the ring on the finger of the bride. "With this ring I thee wed, with my body I thee worship, and with all my worldly goods I thee endow." (p. 304) The idea of worshipping one's wife intrigued me, and caused me to think about the concept of worship.

The word has Anglo-Saxon roots connoting the idea of giving worth or honor. Moreover, worship suggests giving honor to someone or something to whom we attribute worth. In the phrase from the wedding service the groom is, then, promising to give worth and honor to his wife. He is worshipping her in the original sense of the word.

Today we tend to use the word "worship" to describe the praise we give to God, and, since God is our God, our worship signifies the great honor and worth, which is God's due. This represents the Christian understanding, but we need to acknowledge that people worship all sorts of things. The pursuit of wealth and power is given supreme worth by some, so that we can say that they worship money. I believe everyone worships something, but the hidden issue is if that something is worthy of worship. For instance, I once knew a man for whom bike racing was the supreme value in his life. It took precedence over his wife, children, and job. He did not worship his wife, and she eventually divorced him. I understand the appeal of bike racing, but it cannot bear the weight of human worship.

God alone stands worthy of our worship. To be clear, this is the God revealed by Jesus and the God who envelopes us by the Holy Spirit. It follows that we worship God in response to what God has done for us. I John perfectly summarizes it: "We love because he first loved us." (4: 19) God's faithful mercy and compassion for us was fully manifest in the incarnation, ministry, death, and resurrection of Christ. The proper response is worship. Because God astonishingly ascribes to us ultimate worth, we can gladly respond in kind.

Worship, then, stands as basic to our life with God. We cannot avoid it or take it less than seriously. I can assert that for several reasons. First, it helps us orient our lives properly. We need often to be reminded that we are not the Creator, but rather that we are creatures. That perception puts us a long way down the path of living life well.

Moreover, we tend to become like what we worship. Because it is so basic and important we are shaped and molded by the object of our worship. A traditional way of saying this is a Latin phrase: *lex orandi, lex credenda*. Literally, the law of prayer, the law of belief. It basically means this: how and what we pray shapes how and what we believe. And what we believe directly shapes how we act and live. Note the insight that worship precedes doctrine, and the doctrine grows out of our worship of God. There exists a variant of the phrase: *lex adorandi, lex credenda*. Who we adore shapes what we believe.

Worship also shapes our spiritual discipline. To be a disciple implies that we involve ourselves in some sort of ordered living, some kind of regimen. If I am to be a disciple of the piano, for instance, I must practice and study with a teacher. Worship requires that we actually be present at church. It requires our attention and participation. We learn to be disciples for being obedient to the discipline of worship. And this way it prepares us for the discipline of obedience to Christ.

Worship can be and often is private. While driving through the stunning mountains of Montana I sometimes find myself praising and honoring God. But the more important and basic form of worship is both public and corporate. For example, one of the ways we worship happens when we sing hymns. Now, I sometimes do sing hymns by myself, and that act feels like valid worship to me. But singing together with others deepens the experience. It encourages us to know that we together are on the same page, so to speak. We need that sense of being bound together to sustain us.

Worship

In The Episcopal Church we have two main forms of public and corporate worship. They are the Daily Office and the Holy Eucharist. We worship together according to the Book of Common Prayer. In fact, part of what makes a person an Episcopalian is worshiping with other using the BCP. The major service on Sunday is Holy Eucharist. It consists of two parts, Word and sacrament. The Word section comes first, and centers on the reading of the Bible and preaching and praying together on the basis of what has been read. Next comes Communion in which bread and wine are consecrated and then received by the people. These two parts are filled out with prayer, hymns, ceremony, and other forms of music.

The Daily Office consists of Morning and Evening Prayer. These can be used in community or individually. Both services have as their heart the reciting of psalms. Readings from the Bible and canticles (which are usually poetic portions of the Bible that can be sung) and prayers follow.

These are ancient services first developed by monks in the early church. Today all sorts of people use them and they do not require the leadership of an ordained person.

To conclude, I wish to make three remarks about worship. First, worship is about God. That may seem so obvious as to need no mention, but we often get off the track on this. I find too many people who insist that the point of worship is to make them feel better or to inspire them. Others see the point of worship as selling the congregation to potential new members; they want worship that attracts people. In fact, the role of worship is to focus ourselves on God, offering to God our worship, thanksgiving, and our lives.

Second, worship requires our participation. Sometimes people let slip and call the congregation "the audience." And the arrangement of seats in some buildings reinforce that perception. We can think we are there to watch something taking place in the front of the church or perhaps to listen to a public lecture. Worship asks that we give God praise in active ways. We sing and pray. We stand, sit, and kneel. We give our attention and concentration. We walk forward and receive the Body and Blood of Christ at communion. I believe that by the time we have finished worshipping we ought to be tired, because we have given our energy and effort over to God.

Finally, worship asks for our best. It should never become a matter of what we have left over in terms of our energy, time, and finances. Effort and attendance, generosity and preparation are needed if we are to ascribe worth to the one who creates, saves, and sustains us. For instance, I wonder what is going on with people who scramble around to find some pocket change in the offering tray. Is that all God means to them?

I was able recently to attend at concert by the Los Angeles Philharmonic in their stunning home, Walt Disney Hall. They were going to play one of the masterpieces of the twentieth century, the Second Symphony of Jean Sibelius, and one of the giants of the podium, the peerless Herbert Blomstedt, was to conduct. It was worth the expense and energy. The review in the paper spoke of concert as "revelatory," and, indeed, it was. At the end, the audience stood with a roar, shouting bravos. Blomstedt acknowledged the applause, but spent more time pointing to the various musicians who had played important parts of the symphony. Curtain call succeed curtain call. And finally, as the audience stood clapping and shouting, Blomstedt took the musical score from the stand and held it up for all to see, an act I have never seen any other conductor do.

The conductor and musicians gave their best. The performance unfolded as if it were a portrait of human experience. The audience was fully invested in the concert. But at the end, it was the score, the music, that was lifted up. That concert had some of the dimensions of worship to it. In the end, it must be God who is lifted up.

DISCUSSION QUESTIONS

First, have you had a worship experience that changed your life?

Second, how do you prepare yourself for worship?

Three, what part of worship most engenders your relationship with God?

Four, what factors hinder worship for you? What can you do about them?

www.ingramcontent.com/pod-product-compliance
Lightning Source LLC
Chambersburg PA
CBHW051105160426
43193CB00010B/1327